On Screen Directing

On Screen Directing

EDWARD DMYTRYK

FOCAL PRESS
Boston • London

Focal Press is an imprint of Butterworth Publishers.

Library of Congress Cataloging in Publication Data

Dmytryk, Edward.
  On screen directing.

    1. Moving-pictures—Production and direction.
I. Title.
PN1995.9.P7D55   1983   791.43'0233   83–20506
ISBN 0–240–51716–4

Butterworth Publishers
80 Montvale Avenue
Stoneham, MA 02180

10 9 8 7 6 5 4 3

Printed in the United States of America

Contents

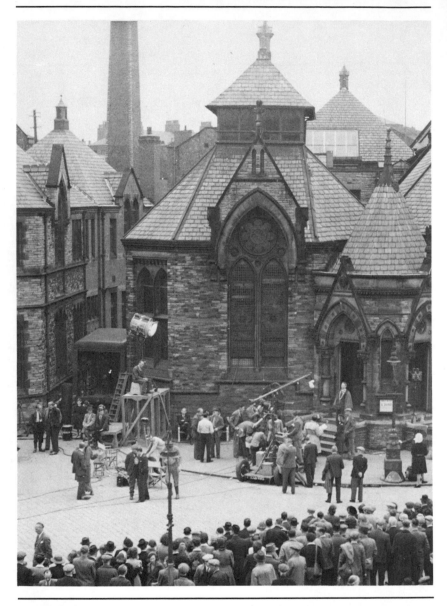

Film as collective art—lighting, sound and camera crews prepare to film British actor John Mills for a scene in So Well Remembered, *this scene taking place in front of the town hall of Macclesfield, England.*

Preface

Leo McCarey, the great comedy director of the thirties and the forties and two-time Academy Award winner, was pleading his case before a banker. He hoped to borrow a million or two for a prospective film. The financier was puzzled, trying to place McCarey in his scheme of things.

"I know what a cameraman does," he said, "he photographs the film. And I know that a scenarist writes the script. Actors, of course, act. But, tell me, Mr.–uh–McCarey?—what does a director do?"

Leo decided to try another bank.

That was long ago, of course. Since then the French have decided to legitimatize that bastard of the arts, the cinema, classifying its various aspects, genres, and occupations, as is their wont; they have pigeonholed the director, or at least some directors, as auteurs, and the screen director is a more familiar figure to the outside world. But, though 90 percent of all film students in hundreds of colleges and universities in the United States and abroad want to be directors, few of them really know what a director does.

A large percentage of the students I have worked and talked with have a vague notion that the director is a kind of artistic dictator who orders the actors to stand here, walk there, or read the lines this way. Very little could be farther from the truth.

To begin with, making a film is both a business enterprise and a collective art. The end result is manufactured as well as created. Most arts, physically, are quite simple; a sculptor and a chunk of marble, a painter and a piece of stretched canvas plus a few tubes of paint, a musician and a piano, a writer with some sheets of lined paper and a pencil. Whether a film is a potboiler or a true work of art, it is necessary to collect a great deal of money, numerous artists from nearly all categories of art, and an even larger group of technicians before a film can really happen.

The director is the person who blends all these various arts and techniques, stirring them in such a way that in the end he achieves a homogeneous piece of work called a film. He must know how to use the various members of the production company, to play them as a composer plays the keys of a piano. He must know how to cozen, to coddle, to flatter, to drive, and to delegate authority without dropping the reins. He must be an expert in logistics; he must remain comfortable while making a thousand decisions a day; he must be willing, even eager, to think and to dream, though the dreams may degenerate into nightmares, twenty-four hours a day, and still retain his sanity.

A reader looking at the table of contents will note, probably with some surprise, that the first half of this book is concerned with script, and with cast and crew relationships. That is about par for the course. On the average, about half a director's total working time will be taken up with preparation. Only then will he be ready to utter those magic words, "Roll 'em! Camera! Action!"

One consideration in reviewing a script is the amount of expensive location shooting that will have to be done. Here Dmytryk directs Robert Ryan in his last film, **Anzio.** *Needless to say, to get such backdrops as the Colisseum, you need to film in Italy, where this picture was made.*

1

In the Beginning

The Script

"In the beginning was the word . . . and the word was God."
Ignoring the sacrelegious use of this biblical phrase when applied
to the average filmscript, writers of all faiths quote Christianity's
favorite apostle when arguing the relative merits of their contributions to the collective art. Hyperbole aside, there is some jus-
tification for their claim. Without a screenplay there is no film.
The real question, however, is, who writes the story that ulti-
mately appears on the screen? And why must a director concern
himself so deeply with his script?

For nearly half a century I have read dozens, sometimes
hundreds, of scripts each year; these are usually written by professional writers. If I found one in a hundred worth making into a
film I considered myself fortunate indeed. One per thousand would
probably be the ratio for a truly exceptional story. This is to be
expected; there are only a few great creators in any field. Yet
almost every writer considers his work the top of the line. Again,
this is normal. Giving birth to a script can be as painful as giving
birth to a baby, and it is often much more prolonged. Find me a
mother who thinks her newborn is ugly. Likewise, what writer
would spend hundreds of hours pounding a typewriter if he thought

the final result would be claptrap? One of the key distinctions between art and most other professions is that the artist must believe in his work; he must "do his thing" whether or not it earns him a penny. A gas station attendant, on the other hand, would hardly pump gas for the sheer love of it. Unfortunately, belief in oneself does not alone an artist make.

Nor does total faith in the value of words make a good motion picture. It merely gives rise to the sort of film we see so often today—what film scholars all over the world call "talking heads." What seems to have been forgotten by nearly all writers, producers, and even most filmmakers is that at its best, the motion picture is not truly a dialogue-writer's medium. It is not a play, although it can effectively present one. It is a medium for images rather than words. After the original story is laid down, many further creative steps can—indeed, should—take place. These steps are usually taken by the director, with the help of a sensitive cameraman, an ingenious cutter, and more often than is realized by the general public, creative actors.

The writer's point of view is necessarily largely subjective; the director must be objective at all cost. (This need for objectivity will be mentioned time and again in the following pages; it is one of the chief attributes of a good director.) The filmmaker will certainly have a subjective preference for certain themes and styles, but he must take a very objective look at how best to present them to the film public. Nothing can kill a career more quickly or certainly than self-indulgence.

No, a script is never "the word of God." Most producers will not consider a script to be final until the director has had his go at it. Unfortunately, that "go" does not always do the job; the average director is no better than the average writer. He can demean as many scripts as he can exalt—maybe more.

The top directors, however, have a few things in their favor. First, a really superior filmmaker usually has a great sense of the visual, the filmic quality of a scenario, if only because his knowledge has been acquired on the field of battle, where his weapons are the camera and the scissors rather than the pen or the typewriter. His favorite quotation is not "In the beginning was the word," but "One picture is worth a thousand words." He can, at least he should always try to, change a sequence in which most of the information is relayed through dialogue into one where the essential message is conveyed through action and reaction. In fact, the ability to make this transformation is what raises a particular director above most of his colleagues.

On another and more common level the director can simplify dialogue through the intelligent use of his camera. The lens can frequently catch in silence what the writer presents in words. Adolphe Menjou once testified that a clever actor can insinuate propaganda into a film with "the lift of an eyebrow, the shrug of a shoulder," and thus subvert a nation's government. The first part of his thesis, at least, is not too far from the truth. Even the atmosphere of a set can often dramatize the essence of a character far better than words. The expression in the eyes of an actor, especially when enhanced by appropriate music, can serve not only to eliminate a whole page of script but to intensify the film's hold on the sensibilities of the audience.

There are three basic sources for film material: the theatrical play, the novel, and the original screenplay. The first of these presents few problems beyond opening up the setting. Inevitably, it remains a play, however good it may be, rather than a true motion picture. The novel and the original screenplay, that is, a scenario written expressly for the screen, are the major sources.

Most film stories are adaptations of novels, and as such confront the adapting writer with the most varied and difficult problems. The average novel is much longer than the average screenplay, necessitating extensive editing and careful selection. If *The Caine Mutiny*, for example, were to be dramatized in its entirety, the film would run 14 to 16 hours, obviously an impossible undertaking.* In actuality, the writer and the director will analyze the theme, the plot, and the characters of the book, and will select those segments that best exemplify what the novelist has to say. (The novel's adaptors may, of course, choose to modify, curtail, extend, or otherwise "improve" the author's point of view.) Once the selections are made they must be arranged in proper sequence (which is not necessarily the order of their appearance in the book), connecting links must be created that will

---

*The development of the miniseries in TV opens up distinct possibilities for full translation of novels into film.

blend the edited portions into a smooth and complete whole, and most difficult of all, essential stream of consciousness passages must be dramatized into visual action.

The third source of film material, the original screenplay, may also present editing difficulties. Most scenes are overwritten, and the director must have a keen awareness of the limits of the audience's attention span, or rather, the limits of its forbearance. A verbose scene can turn off the viewer not only from that particular scene but from the entire film. Attention lost is difficult to recapture. Overstatement in the script implies lack of understanding in the viewer, and no viewer cares to be insulted by being talked down to. I have yet to see an audience that fails to grasp the profundities that exist in even the best film.

One world-famous filmmaker of the thirties and forties worked frequently with an equally acclaimed writer. Few people other than their immediate associates knew the true nature of their collaboration, which went something like this: The writer would present ten or twelve pages of newly written material. The director would scan it, then pick up his blue pencil.

"The opening line is fine," he might say, then he would cross out the next half page. Continuing in this fashion through the rest of the sequence, he would edit it down to about four pages, then return it to the writer with instructions to "smooth out the breaks."

The films they made together were among the best of their time. On the strength of the successes the writer was permitted to direct a couple on his own. They were total disasters, choking to death on their own verbosity.

The example is not exceptional. Directors, too, become blinded by their rewriting brilliance and fall prey to their own arrogance. A prime approach to any work of art is based on humility. Fred Allen, in answer to an interviewer's question concerning the comedian's contribution to his comic material, said, "I write best on dirty paper." That can be a great talent, one that every director should cultivate.

The original screenplay suffers from inadequately developed characterization much more frequently than the novel. The shorter form gives the writer less room for the development of both plot and character, and for some reason plot is favored by most film playwrights. In my opinion, the characters should always be the chief concern. If they are interesting and fully developed, the plot often comes quite easily. Confrontation between two vital human beings is drama, per se. They can be placed in any of a number of situations, and the scenes will almost write themselves. It is commonly accepted that the number of plots is extremely limited, but variety of character is almost infinite. Few people objected to the fact that *West Side Story* was merely a reworking of *Romeo and Juliet*, an old plot indeed. In fact, few were even aware of it. The plot gained new life because the audience was interested in the human beings it portrayed.

The "plot-first" writer usually winds up with a contrived sequence of situations, and most often creates two-dimentional beings whom he can squeeze arbitrarily into his story. It is revealing that the words, "contrived screenplay," have become a cliché with those who make or evaluate motion pictures.

The plot writer is usually concerned with action, which he takes to mean more or less violent movement on the screen. But movement is, or should be, in the mind of the beholder, and a relatively placid scene played by charismatic actors can move the mind of the audience much more than the violent maneuvering of people with whom the audience is not deeply involved. Like a woman in love, intent upon her sweetheart's every gesture, the viewers will be more involved with the way in which a well-developed, sympathetic character moves, sits, or lifts a cup of coffee than they will with the violent antics of someone in whom they have no interest and for whom they feel no empathy.

Given equal development, it is preferable to have actors do things rather than say them—at least whenever possible. "Actions speak louder than words" should be the motto. In this cynical era the viewer knows that people often cover up their real emotions with dialogue. But a person's reaction to a crisis or sudden confrontation, however momentary, can immediately reveal more truth about that person's character than pages of after-the-fact dialogue.

Dialogue—even when not overblown it is often the most difficult problem in a script. Very few writers create true-sounding dialogue, and here I include the rewriting director. Ninety-eight percent of all written dialogue retains a literary flavor. This may work to advantage in the theater, where the poetry of a playwright's words is of primary importance, but for most films it is desirable, even mandatory, that the actors speak in the manner of the characters they represent. Few men or women speak in perfectly organized, polished sentences. One has only to listen carefully to an ad lib interview with a million-dollar-a-year professional athlete, or to a destitute woman being dispossessed of her home, or, for that matter, to the President of the United States in an off-the-cuff press conference to understand that fact. Film dialogue is supposed to be all off-the-cuff. (We will return to this subject again when dealing with acting.)

One caveat concerning script editing. Streamlining a sequence does not mean, as some instructors teach and many writers practice, that no scene should run more than three or four pages. On the contrary, the director often finds himself struggling to merge several short scenes into one continuous sequence. Obviously, besides saving time by eliminating set changes, the greater the length of the scene (within reason), the greater the opportunity to build unbroken mood and emotion. One does not bore an audience with length, but with inane repetition. As long as the signals being sent are fresh, the long scene furnishes a greater sense of smoothness and continuity, and facilitates the manipulation of the audience's attention.

From the practical and logistical point of view there are several aspects of a script that call for careful analysis, particularly if the film must be made expeditiously and at a reasonable cost. Most important is the number of characters in the cast. Within a set time schedule, the greater the number of roles, the less time is available properly to develop all of them. Many films give full coverage to a few leading roles and let the lesser parts fend for themselves. The result is cliché, pasteboard characters who weaken the integrity of the whole. It is often possible and advisable to blend two or more characters into one, thereby furnishing room and time for more complete development of the remaining roles.

It is desirable that all characters, even those only briefly shown, be presented as whole human beings. Any character worth keeping is worth developing, even if it happens to be just the doorman helping a star out of her Mercedes. Allowing him an offbeat remark or a unique bit of action can pique the viewer's interest, enliven an otherwise routine scene, and confirm the humanity of the film's inhabitants. Hitchcock was a past master of this technique. The leading man confronts a loiterer to ask for direction. But the loiterer is such an unusual, albeit believable type and is presented in such an interesting fashion before or after the personal contact, that we wonder about him and his place in the story's scheme of things. As a matter of fact, we will probably never see him again, but his momentary presence has activated movement in our minds and has served to increase our involvement in the film.

The number of locations (including sets) is also a factor that calls for careful examination. Moving a company from one location to another always takes time, even if the shift is merely to another set on the same stage. The more hours spent in moving equipment, cast, and crew, the fewer the hours available for working with the actors on the scenes themselves. In the end, only those scenes, and not the location moves, are the concern of the audience. As in everything to be discussed, there are exceptions, but the benefits of strict location analysis are many, not only in the area of expenditure but in the area of film quality. They should not be ignored.

There is one special technique most writers and filmmakers find difficult to deal with—manipulation of the audience. Every student of the screen knows that films manipulate time and space. So do all narrative arts, although films make these transitions most easily and effectively. But audience manipulation is something else entirely.

Suppose we have two minutes of screen time to convince an audience that character A will accede to a proposition presented by character B. Suppose, further, that the audience knows that A is completely opposed to the proposition, or would normally take much time and thought to arrive at a decision. We have only two minutes; how can we convince our viewers in such a brief time? By manipulating them into accepting that which we want them to accept. There are at least two ways to do this.

First, and probably most common, is type casting—the use of an actor whose appearance and personality make us confident that we know his character. In Hollywood's golden era it was no trick to convince an audience that Clark Gable, or any one of a dozen stars of either sex, could easily and quickly bend anyone to his desires. As a matter of fact, the filmmaker was hard put to keep the audience from wondering why the leading lady did

Location shooting is not the only thing that adds to the cost of the film. Another is the number and elaborateness of the sets required. This set was especially built on R.K.O.'s back lot for the film *Cornered*. Dmytryk discusses the scene to be shot on it with Dick Powell here.

not fall into his arms on sight. But, cleverly manipulated, the audience would swallow acceptance or rejection at the filmmaker's will until the final scene permitted the inevitable.

Second, and much more difficult as well as much more creative, is manipulation by situation. An example furnishes the best explanation. In a Russian film of 1931, *The Road to Life*, directed by Nicolai Ekk, a situation arises that demonstrates this technique most effectively. A gang of young criminals, wild boys of the streets, has been rounded up by the authorities, whose plan this time around is not to put them in jail, where most of them have served repeated sentences, but to rehabilitate them by installing them in a special school in the country. There they can learn to be shoemakers, carpenters, or mechanics. Naturally, none of these young thugs prefers the country to his familiar alleys, and most laugh at the thought of making shoes or building birdhouses. When the pleasant young official from the youth authority puts this proposition to the young hoodlums all hell is about to break loose. But the official calmly pulls out a cigarette case, extracts a cigarette, then extends the open case to the leader of the toughs. Russians are avid smokers, and none of the boys has had a puff since his incarceration. The leader hesitates, torn between animosity and desire. Desire wins. He reaches out and takes a cigarette, an action imitated by other members of the gang. Then comes the clincher.

The official has the only match. He lights his cigarette and blows out the match. Now the burning tip of his cigarette, which he holds between his lips, is the only source of a light. Slowly the gang leader leans forward, then a smile creases his face, and he puffs a light from the official's cigarette. This of course, is followed by similar action on the part of the others, which gives rise to a scene of general hilarity in which three or four boys simultaneously snatch their lights from the official. In the next scene the boys are on their way to the country and we, the audience, are perfectly satisfied that they have freely agreed to go.

Once it has been created, the stratagem is obvious. Taking a light from another person's cigarette, especially when, as in this scene, the cigarettes never leave the smokers' mouths, is an act of intimacy that hardly suffers antagonism. So in the space of a minute or two we rationally accept a decision that in reality might have taken much time and special pleading.

Techniques such as this were highly developed by the Russians, who lost the art when they, like the rest of the world, decided to emphasize dialogue because of its novelty at the time. It would pay us to retreat a couple of generations to recover those aspects of the art of montage, which we could presently use to advantage.

But these examples deal more with creative techniques than with script problems, and it behooves us to move on to other responsibilities of the director.

*Costume design begins early in the production process. Star Carol
Baker here models part of her wardrobe for* The Carpetbaggers.
*At top designer Edith Head presents her design sketches to, coun-
terclockwise, Joe Levine, Marty Rackin and Edward Dmytryk (with
cameraman Joe MacDonald behind him).*

2

To Make Ready

Pre-Production

The director is a problem solver, and problems rarely march in single file. While he and the writer are putting the final touches to the script, which will probably never be quite finished, he will also be selecting a cast and assembling a crew.

The director of experience always has his regulars—men and women of proved worth who have won his confidence through past performance. If the pre-production sequence has progressed smoothly and the budget can afford it, these regulars are already on the roster or standing by. The three persons on whom the director most deeply relies are the cinematographer, the film editor, and the assistant director—not necessarily in that order.

Photography can probably claim a greater percentage of fine artists than any other film craft, with the possible exception of set design. I am not quite sure why this is so, but I do know I have never had a bad photographer on any of the nearly sixty films I have made. They came in different colors, races, nationalities—American, British, Japanese, Austrian, Hungarian, Turkish, South African, and Italian. All were excellent. The rule holds, however; truly great artists are few, and when a director finds one he hangs on to him for dear life.

The exact nature of the cameraman's contributions are discussed in a later chapter. Here it is only necessary to stress that compatibility is of the greatest importance. If an unknown cinematographer is to be employed, it is wise to delve more deeply into his personality than into his professional skills. It is relatively simple to judge his lighting ability by viewing samples of his work; it is not easy to fathom his working personality.

In this situation most directors will seek recommendations from other filmmakers who have used the photographer in question. When doing so, they are advised to keep in mind the working personalities of the directors being questioned. If problems are reported, it is probable that they arose from either side. Only when the enquiring director feels satisfied that he can work harmoniously with the cameraman should final arrangements be made for the collaboration.

Besides supplying his lighting expertise, the cinematographer is often an important factor in maintaining good set morale. To acquire a cameraman is to acquire a family. Just as the director ties a string to his favorite cameraman, so the cameraman insists on keeping his proved aides—camera operator, gaffer, camera grip—who in turn, bring with them their long-time assistants. Thus a large part of the crew stems from the photographer's choice of his right-hand men; he will generally keep friendly but firm control over their on-set behavior.

The film editor (or cutter) usually joins the company a couple of weeks before the start of active production. He is often considered the magician of the crew. Even persons with years of film experience will sometimes marvel at the cutter's skill as he wades through miles of "spaghetti" and emerges with a coherent film. Unfortunately, the supply of excellent editors is not nearly as great as that of cinematographers, for the obvious reason that the best editors are frequently promoted out of their jobs. Most experts in the field consider editing to be the best all-around training for directing, and many of our filmmakers once worked at that job. Unless the director has had a good deal of this kind of experience (and simply watching a cutter at work counts for nothing), he must depend heavily on his editor. When he finds a good one he rarely lets the fellow leave his side.

The cameraman and the cutter are almost always "director's men"—that is, their loyalties are given to the director. It is sad but too often true that the relationship between director and producer is, to use the legal phrase, adversarial. The question of leadership is really the crux of the director-producer relationship. The best film executives have always understood the necessity for the director's on-set primacy and have done everything in their power to strengthen it. They have always been complete delegaters. If they have suggestions, they make them privately and quietly, understanding the director's need to protect his image—both as a leader and as a creator.

The problems most likely to develop on a film, especially one with a long schedule, have two basic causes—first, the conflict of interest that frequently arises between the concerns of business and the demands of art; and second, and certainly more troublesome, the artistic pretensions of a producer who does not feel qualified to direct a film himself but who cannot help trying to inject his creative ideas. It is axiomatic that two generals cannot successfully command one army, and when such a situation arises the director needs all the help he can get. When push comes to shove, numbers count, and the side with the most artists has the greater chance of victory.

I do not speak of winning in the competitive sense, but in terms of artistic integrity. A confident director will listen to suggestions. On rare occasions he may even accept one in its entirety. More often he will discard them because they do not fit his overall conception, with which the suggester is probably not familiar. A suggestion, even when not inappropriate in itself, may muddy values more important to the film. Usually, even the accepted few will be reshaped, perhaps altered beyond recognition, to fit the director's total vision. The chief value of most suggestions is that they may disclose hitherto disguised weaknesses or suggest better approaches, thus forcing the director to explore new channels.

Under any circumstances, openness to suggestion must be carefully controlled, since it can present a number of pitfalls. Some overapproachable directors spend half their time dealing with unsolicited "help." The script clerk, the cameraman, the cutter, even the prop man and the coffee maker have ideas they are eager to share if they see the director floundering. None of them, however, can possibly know the director's total concept. Thus the great majority of these suggestions are probably inappropriate and just waste time. A director with a mind that is too wide open usually has little mind of his own, and is not a competent filmmaker.

And there's the rub. Every member of the crew recognizes indecision and insecurity. If the director exhibits signs of either one of these negative attributes, all of them from the cameraman on down are immediately affected. Morale suffers, and so, obviously, does the film.

In truth, of course, the director is often unsure of himself or of the effects he is hoping to achieve. A director I once worked with (as a cutter) visited the restroom every morning and proceeded to vomit his breakfast. Stage fright usually affects performers for a few hours or even days before their first appearance, but for this director it was a daily visitor throughout the production.

Another example is less tragic and more amusing. Leo McCarey customarily looked back at members of his crew to read their faces for approval after okaying a print. On one film an electrician persisted in greeting McCarey's enquiring gaze with a deadpan wink. "I thought he was on to me," McCarey said. "I had to let him go."

To suffer from butterflies is no sin. Some psychologists suggest it may heighten an artist's performance. But it is a sin to show it to the world. Above all, a director is looked to for leadership, and leadership is what he must demonstrate, even if he has to stage an act of his own.

As will be detailed later, the director should think a number of setups ahead for the sake of continuity. It is also important that he think at least one setup ahead in the interest of crew confidence. When I have completed work on the current setup with "That's great! Print it", I move immediately, without a moment's hesitation, to my next camera location. Using a viewfinder, I indicate the lens to be used, the position and height of the camera, and the preliminary scope of the shot (which may be modified after rehearsal). Then, while the crew is engaged in the usual activity that comes with every change of setup, I collect my thoughts and my actors and prepare to rehearse them for the ensuing shot.

Most intelligent people realize that an artist must do what he thinks best. He cannot present another person's idea with his whole heart and mind unless he has first made it his own. Numerous incidents illustrating this point have occurred over the years. An outstanding example, perhaps apocryphal, involved Howard Hawks and Harry Cohn.

During the period of script preparation the two men had apparently discussed a particular treatment for a certain scene. Hawks eventually shot it, and Cohn viewed it the next day in his projection room. It was not the scene that had been agreed upon. Cohn stormed onto the set and demanded that Hawks restage the sequence as originally conceived. Cool and suave as always, Hawks assured Cohn that he would redo the scene in question the following day. He did, and again Cohn viewed the rushes. It was the same scene, shot for shot, that Hawks had filmed the first time. Again Cohn fumed and again Hawks agreed to reshoot the scene. This he did, exactly as he had shot it the first time and the second time. But now Cohn decided to let well enough alone, and Hawks finished the film on his own terms.

If Hawks had been a lesser director, Cohn might have fired him. If Cohn had been a better psychologist, he would not have made a scene before the whole crew and thus forced Hawks to demonstrate leadership in the only way open to him. Had Cohn discussed the issue in the privacy of his own office, it is quite possible that he and Hawks might at least have reached some acceptable compromise, and Hawks would have reshot the sequence as a "second-thought" effort.

The best executive and the best producer I have known rarely, if ever, vistited the set. Many executives are not that considerate. Under sufficient provocation, directors have had producers removed from the stage; however, the best technique for handling such delicate situations is one that was used by Hawks, that most capable practitioner of "cool." If a producer wandered on the set he was greeted by Hawks with the greatest civility: In his honor, all work ceased, a comfortable chair was quickly provided, and Hawks would engage the visitor in friendly conversation about anything except the scene at hand. It usually took only a few minutes for the producer to realize that his presence was prolonging the schedule, and only his prompt departure could trigger further activity. The prompt departure was always forthcoming.

None of this means that a producer loses all control over his

The producer-director relationship is vitally important to the film. Dmytryk meets with producer Buddy Adler on the 20th Century Fox back lot.

production when the shooting starts. On the contrary, he can be helpful in many ways, and he almost always has an important, sometimes final, say in the editing and certainly in the marketing of the film. Beyond that, many directors can benefit from the tactful control of an intelligent producer. There have been numerous instances of directors gone wild when given total freedom. Even an old hand can become self-indulgent and occasionally run amok. But always, whether it be the producer's or the strong director's, the iron fist should wear a velvet glove.

Ideally, the relationship that the director enjoys with his cameraman and his cutter should extend to his assistant director, and it often does—but not always. Although he bears the title of assistant director and belongs to the Directors Guild, he is not always the director's man. Some independent producers, as well as studio production departments, succeed in making the assistant their man on the set. They can offer incentives and exert pressures to accomplish that end.

The possibility exists because the assistant director is an anomaly. He is not an assistant in the creative sense, but is instead the set foreman. He sees that the set is efficiently organized and that everything the director needs is at hand, whether it be actors, extras, or special equipment; he also marshals the set for the director during rehearsals and shooting. Physically, he works harder and longer than any other member of the crew. He is (or should be) the first one on the set in the morning, oiling the machinery for a prompt start, and he will be the last one to fold up in the evening, since he must do his paperwork after the shooting is finished and make sure that everything is in order for the next day's work. He should also be capable of handling minor crew problems and pacifying troubled actors. If he is exceptionally able he will leave the director free to do nothing but direct. On location, his work and his hours are even harder and longer.

The AD always has at least one assistant, called the second, to help him with his countless chores. He also has the help of the production manager. In many areas their duties overlap. The PM has nothing to do with the daily running of the set or with the handling of the cast, but since he is the main contact between the producer and the set, especially on the business front, he is the chief figure in budgeting, scheduling, and equipment procurement. He also makes all location deals and sets up the location apparatus. It is in this area that a top production manager can make the filming ordeal almost pleasant for the director, or a bad PM can bring it to near or total disaster.

Now that studio back lots have become real estate developments, shooting on location is a part, sometimes a major part, of every film production. These locations may be found in any area of the world, including the North and South Poles. Filming distant locations involves the use of crews, actors, and extras of every race, creed, and nationality, and, of course, company interpreters. Beyond that, these locations are owned or controlled by national, state, or city governments, by corporations, or by private citizens. Representatives of one or all of these entities must be dealt with before a crew can work on any location, and the greatest part of the wheeling and dealing involved in this phase of the production is in the hands of the production manager. Since not all such persons are eager to cooperate with film companies, the PM has to have all the positive qualities of a diplomat as well as a good head for business.

Many locations described in the script cannot be shot as indicated. Large parts of *Doctor Zhivago*, for instance, were shot in Spain. The storm in David Lean's *Ryan's Daughter* was filmed not in Ireland but in South Africa. The North African war scenes in *The Young Lions* were shot in the Borrego Desert in Southern California. Other examples could fill a book.

Selecting locations is customarily the prerogative of the director, although the producer, as guardian of the budget, may have an important part in the process. Once the locations have been picked, a small production group embarks on a reconnaissance tour, one of the more pleasant aspects of filmmaking. The traveling group usually includes the director, production manager, cameraman, and set designer. Interpreters are picked up along the way as needed. Whenever possible, it is also of value to include the screenwriter, since script changes are frequently made to accommodate unforeseen differences in appearance and to use the full potential of the selected locations.

Actual filming always involves tremendous logistical problems, most of which are the production manager's responsibility. At least the key crew members and some equipment must be transported from home base to the location, crews from the host country or, in the United States, the local unions must be hired, as must bit players and extras. Covenient housing must be located and provided for cast and crew. Breakfast and dinner are usually obtained at or near the housing, but lunch and other on-set meals must be catered. Local trucking and personnel transport must also be supplied, as well as the fuel to feed the fleet of vehicles.

Through all this there is the ongoing effort to maintain good relations with the local officialdom and citizenry. Providing the neighborhood's big-wigs with an occasional dinner, a tour of the set, even a company dinner party can work miracles of good will. A truly superior PM knows that a few dollars spent on such entertainment can save thousands of dollars in actual production. Good will is always more economical than a good deal.

The duties of the set and the costume designers are obvious. These artists are almost always competent, talented, and easy to get along with—if their creative integrity is not compromised. They work in special fields with which the director is too often unfamiliar, yet they must have an understanding of the director's basic wishes in their areas. Neither a ballroom nor a gown can be built without the director's signed approval, since he must be sure that the sets and the costumes will not only reinforce the film's character but will fill the needs of the scene's action. There should always be consultation and cooperation among these fields.

The remaining members of the crew have specific jobs, easily identified by their titles. The duties of the electricians, set carpenter, set painter, and set plumber are obvious. As a rule, the last three are not permanent crew members, but report as needed. The set decorator works with the set designer. He dresses the sets and supplies whatever is needed.

The master of properties, or prop man, for short, is in charge of all set dressing that can be easily moved by hand. He furnishes the ashtrays, smoking materials (including an occasional cigar for the director), guns (for Westerns, or almost any film today), luggage, dinnerware, and even the food for scenes that require it—all after consultation with the director. As a matter of fact, the prop man's duties are quite extensive, since he also serves as general factotum for the director, handling the off-set chairs, seeing that the director has his coffee or Coke, and acting as unoffical host to anyone who may visit the set. He takes pride in anticipating the director's every demand, suffering miserably when caught short in any way. That prop men have decided upward mobility is attested to by the fact that John Wayne, the actor, and Henry Hathaway, the director, both started their careers in the prop department. Nowhere else in the film world do prop men come close to matching those in Hollywood. It is perhaps the only craft in which Hollywood is truly supreme.

Among the last, but certainly not the least, is the script supervisor. The title, like many adopted by unions in the vain belief that they will impress employers at bargaining sessions, is misleading. A script supervisor does not supervise the script. She (the script clerk is usually a woman) follows all the action and dialogue shot and makes note of any deviation from the script, records the length of the takes, the camera lenses used, the size of the setups (close-up, medium shot, etc.), and the prints requested by the director. All this information is indispensable to the film editor. More immediately, on the set she must keep track of the wardrobe worn by the members of the cast, their relative positions in any part of a scene, and unusual placing or change of props. She will often cue the actors at rehearsal, and will on occasion tactfully bring the harried director's attention to a missed line or a fouled-up piece of business. (It is surprising how often these things can pass unnoticed.) She is probably more aware of the film as a whole work than anyone on the set except the director. She also often mothers the entire crew.

Some special aides are occasionally useful on a production. Two of these are the dialogue director and the sketch artist, though at least one of these titles is misleading. A dialogue director does not (or should not) direct dialogue. The reasons for this will be explained in a later chapter. Normally, he holds the script and cues actors who may be rehearsing offstage, but I prefer to use a dialogue director as a creative assistant. As with that notorious captain of a ship, the director's postion is a solitary one. While preparing one scene his mind is always occupied in part with the problems of scenes to be shot in the future. It is a permanent state of affairs, since one rarely anticipates a scene without problems. In this situation it sometimes helps to discuss one's doubts and insecurities, along with possible solutions, with the dialogue director. If, during the course of production, he can come up with one or two creative conceptions, even in part, he will certainly have paid his way.

The same holds true for the sketch artist. In my opinion it is a waste of time to have him sketch setups that the director already has in mind. If he can conceive an original pictorial treatment for a future sequence that may be troubling the director, he will earn both the director's gratitude and his salary.

A film's schedule is usually based on its budget, or vice versa. Very few budgets are unlimited. Once the below-the-line cost has been established (and if the director's work habits are known), the production manager and assistant director can set about fixing the schedule. They do this with locations, set space, and actors' contract times in mind. In consequence, the film is rarely shot in script sequence, but in the order that will most economically use the production's funds.

For example, recently an actor was hired for twelve days' work at a cost of three million dollars. Each additional day's work would have cost $250,000. Obviously, this actor's scenes were shot one after the other, regardless of where they fitted into the picture. In Hollywood, an actor is "carried," that is, he is paid for days off between working days, so expensive actors will always be scheduled for continuous shooting. The exceptions, of course, are the leading players, who have run-of-the-film contracts. Players who make a nominal salary need not be scheduled as tightly. It may be more efficient and therefore less costly to carry them while shooting sequences in which they do not appear.

A number of such factors are considered by the PM and the AD. When their version of the schedule is completed and on the board they present it to the director. He will study it carefully, making whatever changes necessary to suit plans his assistants were unaware of. Then he, the PM, and the AD will make a final analysis of the board, and the schedule can be considered set. The fact that the actual shooting almost always veers away from the original schedule is only one more indication of the vagaries of filmmaking.

Setting the schedule is usually the final stage in pre-production. But one area has been purposely ignored here, since it warrants a full discussion of its own. That is, of course, casting of the film.

*Whether to cast well-known stars or unknown actors in a film is a recurring dilemma for the director. For **Broken Lance**, shot in 1954, director Dmytryk, second from left, opted for stars. On this lunch break near Nogales, Arizona he is surrounded (on his right) by Spencer Tracy and (on his left) Robert Wagner and Earl Holliman. Across the table is Jean Peters, Richard Widmark and, with his back to the camera, Hugh O'Brien. The film won an award for being the best Western of that year.*

3

Who's in the Show?

Casting

The cast—it sounds like a throw of the dice, and sometimes it is. But it shouldn't be. Everything so far discussed—the story, the crew, the director—works to one purpose: to bring a group of people onto the movie screen. In one sense this group of people is the single most important element in any film. It must consist of persons who are empathetic, honest, and, in most instances, attractive—well, in all instances, really, since even the brutes and the villains must attract the audience's interest and attention. The selection of this group of people that we call the cast must be as much a work of art as any other activity involved in the making of a film. For a number of reasons it is of greater concern to the director than to anyone else involved in the production. Let us approach the problems of casting in proper order. First, the stars.

In most productions the top two or three players are of interest not only to the director, but to the producer or producing company, to the distributor, and to the exhibitor. Consequently, each seeks input into the selection. In many instances a film cannot be sold to an exhibitor unless, as he frequently puts it, he has some "names" to place on his marquee. The director may feel that a certain, as yet undiscovered actor could play the leading role to perfection, but the producer, with the exhibitor in mind, will object that the actor in question has no drawing power. Nine times out of ten he will be right. It takes time and money to sell a new actor to the public, both in terms of career and in terms of one film. The audience rarely cottons to a newcomer unless he or she has an especially winning part in an especially powerful story. There just are not too many of these. There are, however, a few men and women who can carry even a mediocre film. These are the true and only stars, and for necessary and sufficient reasons. They have a combination of all the required qualities, which means they are usually physically attractive, they project strong personalities, they are "loved by the camera," and they can act. It is one of Hollywood's myths that many top stars are beautiful or handsome, but not very talented. Obviously, that is sheer nonsense. Spencer Tracy was handsome, and many critics also considered him to be the world's finest actor. The same can be said for Paul Newman or Robert Redford, for Jane Fonda or Vanessa Redgrave, as well as a number of others. Any director would accept one or more of these in almost any film. The producer and the exhibitor would be equally delighted.

The point is that casting the top roles is almost always a collective decision in which the director may have to compromise his predilection for art and integrity. In most instances the problem is not insurmountable, and the compromise is painless.

Occasionally, however, a film of unusual quality requires "new faces."* Established actors undoubtedly bring their unique personalities to each part they play. A Bogart part is just that; however well acted, it is a Bogart part. (There are exceptions.) The "new" actors also bring their personalities into their screen characterizations, but the audience, who has no previously established image to refer to, accepts the unknown actors as true representations of the people they play. These "new faces" often go on to highly successful careers and their screen personalities become as fixed as those of established stars. There are many

---

*I put new faces in quotation marks because most discoveries are not truly new. The majority have been learning and practicing their craft for years, and have a world of experience when they are finally "discovered." Ben Kingsley, the star of *Gandhi*, is a case in point.

examples of such overnight discoveries—Dustin Hoffman in *The Graduate*, Richard Dreyfus in *American Graffiti*, several of the young men in *Breaking Away*. The examples go on and on.

Discoveries of this kind are not equivalent to finding a beautiful face and a sexy body at a soda fountain. Those are personalities, discovered first and then inserted into what the discoverers hope will be successful debuts and eventually, rewarding careers. Sometimes it turns out they can also act.

With a few exceptions, two or three of these star names are about all the marquees and the advertising media can accommodate with comfort. It is also just about all the film's dramatic needs can accommodate if good taste and cinematic integrity are held in any regard. On occasion, in an attempt to build a blockbuster out of a weak or uncertain script, a producer will pack his cast with stars, many playing bit parts, which, in an effort to support the name actors and justify the added expense, are called vignettes. Almost without exception this only serves to make the audience aware of the mechanics of manipulation. Really good, appealing films need no such bolstering. On the contrary, over the years many fine and successful films have been stocked with good actors, but with no name players at all.

Now back to the everyday average film. The farther one works down the roster of players, the greater the director's freedom of choice, since the supporting cast, however important to the film, is not a major concern to the distributor. Though most producers continue to contribute to the casting process, as a rule their role becomes an advisory one.

The director who feels strongly about picking his own actors must know what constitutes good screen acting. Many actors, as well as most nonprofessionals, think the only difference between acting for the stage and acting for the screen is voice volume or intensity. This is demonstrably not so. It is true that there is no such thing as a stage whisper on the screen, but there are many other differences between the techniques. More than one Broadway actor making his or her film debut has asked me, "Where is my audience? Do I play to the camera, to the crew, or to you?"

My answer, of course, is, "None of these. First of all, you don't 'play' at all. You do not give a 'reading,' or a 'performance.' You talk to, and with, the other actor (or actors) in the scene, and only to him. When you need to shout you shout; if you want to whisper, you whisper—really whisper. You look at the actor you're talking or listening to. You do not favor an imaginary audience or the camera. You do not have to worry about the audience seeing you. There is no advantage to upstaging in films, and only the beginner will attempt it. The camera will move to pick you up no matter which way you face. And if you have a funny line you do not wait for the laugh; a cold audience may leave you with egg on your face."

Acting for the screen is essentially naturalistic; acting in the theater is not, although the finest performers can make it seem so. But it is really similitude; it has to be, because of the nature of the theater. If an actor on the stage whispers "I love you" to his sweetheart, he must be heard at the back of the balcony. It is difficult to half-shout "I love you" and make it intimate. But the screen actress can whisper "I love you" in her lover's ear, and if he can hear it, the microphone will pick it up.

Even more important, if the camera is focusing on her in a tight over-shoulder shot, she had better mean it. Acting for the screen is really a matter of being—not behaving. Honest attitude is everything. The screen actor has to listen authentically to his vis-a-vis, unless, of course, inattention is called for. He does not listen for a cue; he may never get it. He must hear all that is being said, and show that he understands it—and that means show it in his eyes. John Ford once said to John Wayne, while keeping a firm grip on the Duke's chin, "Act with your eyes, not with your face!" Another poet said, "The eyes are the windows of the soul." Although the biologists tell us that eyes are simply organs with no expressive power of their own, we all know it isn't so. One look at a Katherine Hepburn close-up will convince even the most skeptical scientist.

One of the chief demands on an actor is that his speech and his actions always appear spontaneous. To the audience, the events and conversations on the screen are taking place for the first time, and at the very moment it is viewing them. The great actors have the gift of seeming to bring their reactions or their speeches out of their minds at the moment they are reacting or speaking. They have the ability to phrase a line so that it appears to be truly spontaneous. This may crush the writer who wrote it, but who would have it any other way?

With all this and more in mind, the director casts his players on the basis of his familiarity with their work, the films he has seen, recommedations of his colleagues or the players' representatives (agents), and occasionally, personal interviews. He tries to find actors who can be the characters as he originally visualized them. The longer he plays around with his characters, however, the more he is inclined to take chances, to experiment, to look for a new twist to his on-screen people. Often an interview with an actor will disclose interesting side characteristics, either in appearance or in attitude. Sometimes, the director purposely seeks to off-cast a part.

It is relatively safe to choose a player on the basis of past performance. It may also result in a "safe," routine characterization. Taking a chance, when it is successful, adds many a plus to a film's effectiveness. Dick Powell, the sweet-singing tenor in many Warner Brothers musicals of the thirties, was an unexpected success as Phillip Marlow in *Murder, My Sweet.* He turned out to be just the offbeat type the character needed, and many critics, as well as Raymond Chandler, the author of the Marlowe novels, named him the best Phillip Marlowe in Hollywood, though the character was subsequently played by superior actors. Similarly, casting tough guy Humphrey Bogart as the psychotic and vulnerable Captain Queeg in *The Caine Mutiny* was a stroke of near genius for which Stanley Kramer deserves full credit. As a matter of fact, most of that film's casting was offbeat, including former "pretty boy" Van Johnson as the earnest, not-too-bright executive officer and Fred MacMurray as the cowardly intellectual.

Occasionally, off-casting becomes a stunt, an inside joke. Mike Mazurki as Don Juan may be worth a few laughs in the director's office, but it will bring only tears at the box office. How the director casts his film should depend in part on what he feels the audience will accept, or what he thinks he can make them accept—more than accept—take warmly to heart. Basically, that means they must love to love the protagonists and love to hate the antagonists. The audience is the key to good casting, as it is to good story telling. Every good director tries to make the film he thinks is worthwhile, but if he cannot make his viewers feel that his film is worth experiencing, he is only making home movies.

Important considerations for the director in casting a film are the work habits of the actors—and how well he works with them. Here Dmytryk enjoys a light moment with stars Robert Mitchum and Peter Falk, along with an unidentified jeep driver, while filming Anzio.

The director's techniques for working with actors are discussed later, but here I must again bring up the question of compatibility. Getting the best performance is often a highly emotional experience, both for the actor and the director. The two do not always see eye to eye, either in the area of characterization or that of technique. One actor's working habits may be antipathetic to those of his fellow artists. Conflict may sometimes give rise to great art, but in a process as complex as filmmaking, harmony can be a blessing.

Just as the director investigates his cameraman's working personality, so he must look into the characters and predilections of his players. There have been numerous instances of major strife caused by extreme differences in actors' working habits. For example, Glenn Ford is a professional. Like all true professionals, he prepares at home rather than on the set at the expense of the company's time. He is at his best and most spontaneous in the first few takes. Marlon Brando, a great actor, does not know what he wants to do until he has tried a variety of approaches. Before I cast him for *The Young Lions*, a director who had worked with him told me, "He can be quite dreadful for seventy takes, then there is take seventy-one and, suddenly, magic!" But by take seventy-one Ford was used up and dry. This difference in techniques led to an open battle on the set of *The Teahouse of the August Moon*, and the film suffered.

The cast of *The Young Lions* included Brando and Montgomery Clift. Clift presented problems of his own, but shooting numerous takes was not one of them. He was at his best in take one or two. Fortunately, he and Brando never shared a scene, so the difference that might easily have caused a shutdown never arose.*
Vincent Sherman once made a film with Bette Davis and Miriam Hopkins, two of Hollywood's more headstrong actresses. I asked him whether he had enjoyed directing them. "I didn't direct them," he said. "I refereed." So these factors must be carefully considered if one is truly to be the director of a film and not a referee. A few actors of both sexes have an inclination to take over the production, to be "king of the hill." This tendency, too, must be guarded against, but more on this later.

---

*Let me say, however, that Brando grew to understand and appreciate the film. In consequence, his work habits improved tremendously, and for the greater part of the film he worked efficiently and with real dedication.

Casting bit parts presents its own problems. This duty is left completely in the director's hands and it, too, is enlarged on in a different context. Unless special types are called for, the casting of extras is routine. They are supplied by central casting in the number required, and their disposition is usually left in the hands of the assistant director.

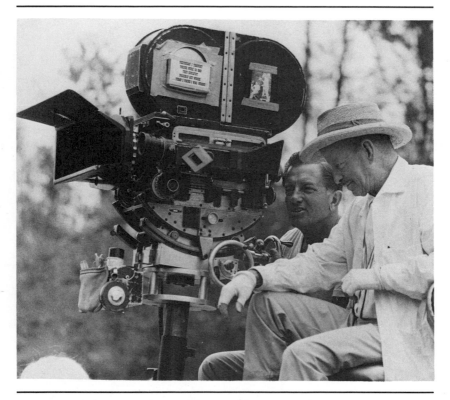

Dmytryk here works with one of his favorite cameramen, Joe MacDonald, whose sense of humor often saved the day during troublesome times. The film is **Alvarez Kelly.**

4

Working with the Crew

Everyone wants credit—the neighborhood postman, the local butcher, the county coroner, the ambassador at large, and certainly every member of a film crew. I do not mean the quick flash of a name on a theater screen; I mean credit from co-workers, family, and perhaps most of all, from superiors, especially the boss. The intelligent sharing and dispensing of credit can be one of the director's most rewarding investments.

The director should study every man and woman on his crew, just as he will study each member of his cast. Since each individual reacts differently to outside stimuli, the director must subtly vary his approach to all crew members if he is to get their maximum output. Just as one individual differs to some degree from every other individual, so does each crew as a unit differ from others. This is most evident when working with crews of different nationalities.

The members of an English film company, for instance, have a strong sense of dignity and personal rights. Woe to the director who violates these sensibilities. He can, and probably will, be sabotaged in the most subtle and ingenious ways. Like most Spaniards, the Spanish worker has his pride, which must be respected even if the director does not know what the man is proud of. The German crew respects a strong hand, while the Italian worker will feel you don't love him if you don't shout at him— his mother always did. (Incidentally, he will give you plenty to shout about.) But the Hollywood crew is unique. As a unit it is still probably the best in the world and, perhaps because its members are so highly paid, it will suffer a great deal of nonsense.

Only under the most extraordinary circumstances will an English crew allow even a few minutes of overtime; the American crew will work indefinitely long hours. It is only necessary that its members be adequately fed and paid (and the overtime rates can be staggering). The Hollywood crewman also has a high insult threshold. He will overlook snobbishness and sarcasm, and smile tolerantly at the director's incompetence. As long as his union agreement is respected and he is paid well for his work, he will do his job competently. If more than competence is desired, it must be earned.

From the start the director must inspire confidence. He must behave with assurance; he must make quick, positive, and lasting decisions. Most important of all, he must be secure enough to delegate duties and to allow the workers to complete those duties in their own fashion, even if it offends his idea of efficiency. One of the most difficult things to learn is how to stand by while a subordinate performs some operation in a "different" way.

Henry Hathaway's "short fuse" was notorious. Once, seeing a laborer carrying a wooden plank in an unorthodox manner, he screamed, "Damn it! That's not the way to carry a piece of lumber!" Jumping up from his chair, he grabbed the plank from the surprised man's grasp and demonstrated his own mode of portage. Hathaway had rough sledding when he started directing, but his crews learned to love him for his eccentricities and to laugh at his screaming.

The auteur theory notwithstanding, no director makes a film on his own. He needs the help of every member of his crew—and, in an important sense, each member has equal standing. A Rolls Royce cannot run efficiently if even one $1.25 spark plug is missing; a production will not run smoothly if a single worker fails at his job. If there is one crewman whose work is not vital, he should not be on the set. He is excess baggage, and that costs extra.

Only results count. If they are satisfactory, the ends justify the director's patience, the ends in this case being increased crew morale, cooperation, and efficiency. If the director can condition his crew so that each member, no matter what the size of his contribution, can go home at night and say to his wife, "Honey, wait till you hear what happened on *my* picture today," the director will reap the benefit. If the film is successful, the director will get most of the credit.

In his choice of pictorial treatment, the director deals primarily with one person, the cinematographer. The lighting cameraman will have his own ideas concerning mood and style after he reads the script, and they will usually match those of the director. But the very richness of the English language makes it susceptible to ambiguity, and it is vital that the director discuss his conception with the cameraman. Sometimes this can be done simply, by citing examples from other films. If the director hopes to obtain original effects, however, he must resort to other references. I prefer to show my cameraman a book of paintings by some artist who has captured at least a large part of the mood and style I hope to achieve. I may refer to Degas, Renoir, or, for a medieval background, Caravaggio. For *Murder, My Sweet*, which has become a prototype for the genre now known as *film noire*,* I chose Daumier.

The cameraman will quickly understand the director's intention and, if he is an artist, he will embellish, or simplify, or heighten the style with contributions of his own. As always, when working with a more-than-competent creator, the final result will be not so much what the director wanted, but what he wishes he had wanted. No one can ask for more.

It has been stated that the cameraman is always a member of the location selection crew. His presence is necessary not only because he must see the locations in order to estimate the type and amount of equipment needed for adequate lighting, but because he must note the position of the greatest light source of all, the sun. It is important that he learn when and where it rises, when and where it sets, and its course across the heavens between these two extremes. He must also extrapolate these factors to the actual date of shooting, since they vary with the time of year. A well-lit composition today may be in complete shadow a month from now. It pays to be aware.

The sun's path also dictates the number of daylight hours. In the northern latitudes—say, New York, Rome, or Madrid—sum-

---

*The term *film noire* translates literally from the French as "black cinema."

The cameraman likes to choose his camera operator, who in turn likes to select his own crew. Here, on location in France for the filming of **The Mountain***, Dmytryk discusses a scene with cameraman Franz Planer (center) while camera operator Til Gabani listens in from the ladder above.*

mer will add as much as six hours to each shooting day. London, Berlin, and Paris have an even greater time differential. It would seem to be the better part of common sense to schedule location work for the summer months, but factors other than light are often more important. When film locations are shot in winter, either the cost of shooting goes up or the time and the quality of shooting go down. Such Alice-in-Wonderland decisions are hard to debate, but the director should always keep seasons in mind.

Communication is another very important consideration, especially on foreign locations. In his own homeland, a director must only put up with the inconsistencies of his own tongue. On alien ground he must deal with another language; therefore unless he is completely fluent in it, he should have an interpreter. I do not mean a local interpreter, no matter how well he speaks the director's language. I mean an interpreter from the director's bailiwick, who will at all times be the director's man. Why? Let me cite an example.

For work in Hong Kong I took along a Chinese friend to be my ears. We employed Hong Kong interpreters (standard procedure) who understood and spoke English perfectly. For the sake of protocol and labor relations, I always relayed instructions to our Chinese crew and cast through one of these men. My friend always listened in, and in a surprisingly large number of instances he would report, "He (the interpreter) did not say what you asked him to say."

Blame it on the ambiguity of language, or on the fact that almost everyone knows how to do it better than the director does, whatever it is, but this problem is universal. Whether the language was Italian, Hungarian, or Hebrew, local interpreters were frequently inexact, and I was always thankful for the presence of my own linguists, who would keep us all at it until understanding was complete.

Shooting on a distant location presents other special problems, not only in working and communicating with the crew but in selecting it. Here, the director, the production manager, and the assistant must exercise special care.

A crew away from home can resemble soldiers in foreign climes or tourists abroad. Occasionally, the rules of decorum that prevail on home grounds will be abrogated, which can lead to production

slowdowns and added expense. To many people outside of southern California, people from Hollywood are visitors from outer
space. Though the citizens of a distant town may be very hos-
pitable, they are constantly on watch, and the embers of suspicion
can quickly be fanned into the fires of xenophobia. At all times,
tact is of the greatest importance, and so is proper, and legal,
behavior. For years after the filming of *Around the World in
Eighty Days*, Paris was virtually off limits for Hollywood productions because Mike Todd had towed citizens' modern cars off
the streets at night without first getting permission from the
authorities. He "fought and ran away" successfully, but the vis-
iting productions that followed him paid heavily for his
transgressions.

Excessive drinking, drug taking, or anything that diminishes
or distorts rational behavior can be a serious problem, even if the
company is isolated in the desert. For example, on one such
location our wardrobe man proved to be a heavy drinker. During
studio shooting, when he went home every night, he was harm-
less and a good worker. Away from home and mother it was a
different story. Every evening after dinner he became a holy terror, bothering actors, fighting with fellow crewmen, and letting
me know where I had goofed during the day's shooting. There
was no time for gentle, sympathetic treatment. After a few days
he was replaced.

Malingering can also be a problem, even on a nearly perfect
Hollywood crew. Another production of mine was scheduled for
several weeks' work in the French Alps. A few days before our
departure from Los Angeles, the crew was assembled and the
difficulty of the work was laid out carefully and positively. That
would include shooting near the top of Mont Blanc, daily climbing to locations well off the beaten paths, and filming on nearly
vertical, snow-covered slopes. Our day's schedule would usually
start with a hike up steep mountainsides, lasting from a half-
hour to two hours. Coming back downhill in the late afternoon
would be hardly less arduous.

Each member of the crew was questioned individually. All felt
eager, healthy, and challenged—or so it seemed until we were in
the Alps and ready for our first climb. I had picked a young man
as script clerk because I thought he could stand the conditions
better. How wrong I was. On the day before shooting started he

disclosed that he had lost the toes of one foot in Korea. My sympathy for his handicap was completely eclipsed by my anger at his deliberate dishonesty. He had obviously tricked us into a free trip to Europe, Paris, and the Alps, knowing he could not make the slightest effort at climbing.

Fortunately, the company included a female secretary who had had considerable experience as a script clerk for David Lean. She took over immediately and made every climb with little difficulty and no complaints. We might have had a serious and costly delay before a replacement could arrive. So much for chauvinism—and Chapter 4.

Although much of **The Mountain** *was shot on location in the Alps, this scene is a close-up shot on a set at Paramount Studio which was later inserted into an outdoor sequence. Spencer Tracy is the mountaineer.*

5

It Ain't Necessarily So

Set Design

No examination of the problems of pre-production is complete without a discussion of set design. Sets, as distinct from locations, are an indispensable part of almost every film. In this area the director has many options, and therefore many decisions to make.

He can choose between live (or actual) sets and those constructed on the stage. He can opt for expansive and expensive sets, or he can make do with the simplest possible construction. He can build complete, fully detailed sets, à la D. W. Griffith or C. B. De Mille, or he can ask for minimal sets fleshed out with matte shots, miniatures, forced perspective, or a combination of any or all of these.

He can also vary the size of the set required. If, for instance, the director has a short scene—say, one of four or five pages— he can diminish the scope of the staging and shoot against two walls instead of three. Eliminating a single wall can save thousands of dollars. This is a small sample of the application of the law of diminishing returns. The question is simply this: Does one lose more in value by somewhat limiting the scope of the short scene than is gained in dollars by limiting the size of the set? The loss in dramatic value may be so minor as to be unnoticeable; the dollars gained may be better spent in expanding a more important set, or in affording extra time for shooting a particularly crucial scene. To put it another way, building the third wall may well be merely an exercise in self-indulgence that adds nothing of real value to the scene. If the director is conscientious he will resort to the law of diminishing returns many times during the course of production.

Of course, many other factors must be taken into account when choosing sets. Let us consider the simplest form of the problem—a standard interior such as a large living room. It would be quite possible to find a satisfactory room of this sort in some private residence. But what are the advantages or disadvantages of such a locale as compared to a set built on the studio stage?

The chief, and perhaps only, advantage is expense. Such a room could be leased for immeasurably less than it would cost to construct a similar one on the stage. Some directors might consider the reality of the live set another advantage. Against these is arrayed a long list of disadvantages, of which a few are as follows:

1. Great care must be exercised when working on a live set. It is usually private property, and any damage would be inconvenient to the owner and costly to the production. The extra care necessarily involves extra time.
2. Lighting is much more difficult and probably not as effective, since freedom of lamp positioning is decidedly limited and installing overhead lighting next to impossible.
3. Space is severly restricted. There are no "wild" walls, and the camera, its tripod or crab dolly, the lights, and the personnel necessary to manipulate all this equipment must be accommodated within the room itself, leaving little space for staging the action.
4. Movement and variety of setups are severly limited, as is any possibility for shooting in more than one direction.
5. Heat and ventilation problems become acute, as does access to the set.
6. The expense of transporting cast, crew, and equipment to the room's location decidedly diminishes the savings in set cost.

Against these must be placed the following advantages of the stage set:

1. It can be planned and built exactly to the director's specifications and, since it will be designed by an architect with a special ability to develop the set's visual and dramatic potentials, it can be at least as real as any live set. In fact, where special character is of importance, such as aging or dilapidation, the stage set can look more real than any live one in existence.
2. There is much more freedom of crew action; nothing of special value has to be protected for a concerned owner.
3. The cameraman enjoys complete lighting freedom. Normally, there are no ceilings, and overhead lighting is standard. (Ceilings can be quickly rigged for setups that demand them.)
4. All walls are "wild," that is, they can be taken out when additional room for camera setups is desired and can be replaced when needed.
5. All equipment can be kept off the set. For a long shot, even the camera can be positioned outside an open end.
6. The director can take full advantage of the whole set in staging his scenes. Movement of actors is limited only by its four walls, not by lights, camera, or personnel.
7. The absence of a ceiling and the presence of stage air-conditioning make working conditions more pleasant and the work correspondingly more efficient.
8. Time on the set is not limited by the needs and demands of private owners, or of their near neighbors.
9. The power supply is unlimited. No special electrical sources or generators are required.

Perhaps the single greatest advantage of the stage set is that it can and should be designed to specifically enhance character, create mood, and further the overall concept of the film. The odds against finding a live set that would perfectly satisfy all these requirements are staggering.

As the set grows larger, however, the comparative advantages decrease. Strictures of space, lighting, and accessibility are di-

Much of The Caine Mutiny *was shot aboard a Navy destroyer, but this wardroom was built on a stage at Columbia Studio to match the real thing. Dmytryk and Stanley Kramer listen as the Navy chief technical advisor briefs Fred MacMurray, Van Johnson and Humphrey Bogart.*

minished in the live set—say, a banquet hall or a sports arena—and the greatly increased cost of building such a large set from scratch tips the balance against it. In the extreme, of course, if the director wants to shoot the Colosseum he must go to the Colosseum. Or must he?

Today's filmmakers are often spoiled. Unlimited funding can be a blessing, but it can also diminish the need for ingenuity and anesthetize the creative senses. Working with a skimpy budget can sometimes evoke miracles of improvisation—yes, and of art.

I was making my third film as a director, a B movie called *Golden Gloves*. As the title suggests, many of the scenes had to be staged in a prizefight arena. I hoped to hire the Hollywood Legion Stadium and 3,000 extras; the B budget allowed me an empty stage and 300 bodies.

When I had absorbed the shock, I started to study the real thing. I noticed the arena house lights were on only between rounds; while the fighters were working, the ring was brightly lit from overhead and the house lights were dimmed. This, along with clouds of cigar and cigarette smoke, make it impossible to see anything beyond the ring, except. . . . There lay the solution. We would use the long shot only when a round was in progress. Not only would the attention of the audience be entered on the fighters, but the rear of the stadium would be in relative darkness.

Setting up the long shot, I placed the 300 extras, minus twenty or thirty, in the shape of a triangle between the camera and the ring, with the apex of the triangle at the camera. The people on the sides of the triangle just overlapped the edges of the frame; nobody was wasted. When we were ready to shoot, the lights over the ring brightly backlit the spectators between the ring and the camera. Grips ran through the small crowd with bee-smokers, filling the set with a smoky haze.

Then came the "except. . . . " At the back of the stage, far beyond the ring, black draperies had been hung from ceiling to floor and stretched from wall to wall. In front of the draperies, rostrums of varying heights had been placed at odd distances across the stage. On each rostrum sat two or three extras, taken from the small group we had set aside, each armed with flare matches. These extras could not be seen in the dark, but during the shooting of the scene they would, from time to time, at random, light their flare matches, which were bright enough to photograph. The effect on the screen was of a couple of thousand fight fans, invisible in the darkness, except when occasional smokers lit their cigarettes* (Figure 1).

At any cost the scene would have been original and arresting. At its actual cost, it was exceptional. Effects of this sort can frequently be achieved through a wide assortment of means. Film affords the filmmaker almost endless opportunities to create— to deceive the audience, if you will, but to deceive it to its advantage. That is the essence of creativity, whether in filmmaking, painting, writing, or, let us say, dancing. Did Nijinsky really pause in midflight? Of course not. But he moved in such a way that the audience believed he did, and exulted. Through creative deception the artist distills the essence of life, situation, or character, and shows his audience truth, free from extraneous or obfuscating detail. In an art that is also a business, he can also save a buck.

Another example of money-saving technique, borrowed from Murnau, involved the use of a set built in forced perspective. In *So Well Remembered*, a film made in England, a scene called for staging on the crowded terrace of the House of Commons. The terrace was not available for filming, however, and since it is extremely long, duplicating it would have demolished the budget. I could, of course, have shot across the terrace, but the scene would have lost all of its inherent effectiveness.

The art director came up with a wonderful idea. His plan called for some forty or fifty feet of the terrace, as seen along its length, to be built to full scale. Beyond that, the perspective would be so forced that the succeeding couple of hundred feet could be depicted in about thirty. It meant bringing the sides and the floor of the terrace together at decidedly sharp angles.

But there was a hitch. How could we populate the diminishing section of the terrace? The solution was not all that difficult. Furniture—tea tables and chairs—was built, also in perspective and in diminishing proportion. To occupy the chairs, I selected a number of extras, ranging in size from near average for the forepart of the perspective section of the set through people of progressively decreasing stature until, farthest from the camera,

---

*This effect can be so spectacular that in recent years it has often been used in outdoor stadia as part of the half-time entertainment at night football games.

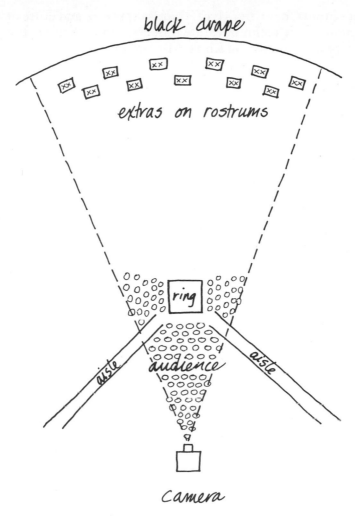

Figure 1

the smallest midgets were seated. Shot from the only position possible for the desired effect, the terrace appeared to stretch away from the camera for hundreds of feet and, magically, the people occupying it were all of normal size.

No matter how it is done—with shadows, forced perspective,

paper cutouts, or mirrors (yes, that is done too, and quite often)—
the more such techniques are understood and used, the more
effective and engrossing films will become.

Once the shooting starts, the director is the man in charge and must know what he wants. Here Dmytryk directs actor Gregory Peck in Mirage.

6

The Shooting Starts

The start of a film brings stage fright, insecurity, and some indecisiveness; which is to say it is no different from an opening night in the theater, the first round bell in a prize fight, the first charge of a fighting bull, or the first minute of a football game. Everyone on the set feels it, although it probably affects the director and the actors more than members of the crew. I have never made a film without wishing I could reshoot the first few days' work. The problem, then, is how to counteract the weakness of the average beginning.

There are valid reasons for this problem. The first is psychological, the second quite practical. Even when the director is familiar with most of his crew, there will always be a few individuals whom he knows only superficially, if at all. Many of the actors will be total strangers, regardless of the brief meetings at casting interviews. No matter how conscientiously the director has tried to get acquainted with the new members of both cast and crew, he has had no opportunity to know them under fire. The differences between off-set and on-set behavior are often startling.

So, like a good boxer during the first round of a fight, the good director spends a measurable amount of time in feeling out his coworkers. This detracts from total application to the business at hand, and he may overlook a number of the little things that go to make up a day's work. The same can be said for cast and crew.

There are several ways to deal with this bothersome period. Perhaps the best is to schedule walk-throughs for at least the first two or three days. By walk-throughs I mean action scenes of no special dramatic content. For instance, an actor might drive up into the foreground of a shot, get out of his car, and as the camera pans with him, walk into a building. There might be shots of an actor, or actors, roaming the city streets; or, as in most suspense films, a series of silent setups taking our hero through a series of dimly lit sets as he proceeds to a fateful rendezvous.

Such scenes, whether shot on location or on the stage, are not, as a rule, too demanding of the player and are relatively easy to stage. There are usually several in a script, though logistical requirements might permit only a few of them to be moved to the head of a schedule board. This ploy also takes advantage of the fact that an audience is not nearly as critical of action scenes as it is of dramatic confrontations, in which the actors should be at their best. Two or three days of such work can shake down the entire company. The director, the cast, and the crew can get rid of their butterflies and be ready to settle down to serious filmmaking.

If the schedule does not offer enough of such action to fill the necessary two or three days, another gambit may prove satisfactory. Holding full, though casual, rehearsals of the first few scenes on the schedule can easily occupy the required breaking-in period. Although the production department may scream at the apparent loss of time, that time will usually be recovered because of the increased confidence of those who make the film.

It must be remembered that the schedule is not a constitution; it is merely an estimate, a hope. It is safe to say that not one film in a hundred moves exactly to schedule. It can also be safely said that probably as many films come in under schedule as over schedule. Like almost everything else in these days of computer science, the schedule is a statistical approximation, nothing more.

What is not statistical is the desire to get the best possible scenes on film, and the secret of accomplishing that lies in the director's ability to get the best possible performances out of his cast.

"What does the director do?" Many directors besides Leo McCarey have been asked that question. At the university I hear it nearly every day. A full answer would take a week. The simple answer is, "He makes the actors feel completely secure." That is the ideal, rarely reached. But the closer the director approaches that ideal, the nearer he is to the perfect film. Instilling security, however, is not an easy matter.

Before shooting starts the director should meet his actors as often as necessary. The necessity in question is agreement on characterization. For obvious reasons, there will usually be little difference of opinion. Good actors are also intelligent persons. If the characters and the situations are written to be understood by the average theatergoer, as they should be, they will certainly be understood by the actors at first reading. After all, understanding character is their business.

As previously noted, however, meanings can be ambiguous, equivocal, or even inconsistent. An actor may sometimes be puzzled by an apparent contradiction in his screen character as it is depicted in two different scenes of the script. A few words with the director will usually clear up the problem. The actor will realize that an alternative interpretation of one of the scenes will allow it to square with the other. As his confusion subsides, his grasp of the character grows, and his insecurity diminishes. However, if this concern applies to a number of scenes in the script, a review of the story as a whole is in order. If what the director saw as a clean, straight-line story can be confusing to the actor, it will undoubtedly be confusing to the viewer. The director should then set to work with the writer, or on his own, to clear up the ambiguities.

In the interests of economy, efficiency, and performance, such problems should be eliminated before the production goes on the floor. The actor must have time to immerse himself in his role long before he plays his first scene.* If he knows clearly what the director expects of the character and agrees with that conception, he will function at a higher level of awareness and security. The key word here is security.

The insecure actor will give a safe performance—and it will be just that, a performance. (Though I use the word performance frequently in this book, it must be understood that I do so for

---

*This suggestion also applies to the bit player who is cast after the production is well under way. He should always be given a few days before he reports on the set to get into his role, however small.

lack of a better word to describe the end result of a screen actor's work. In a film, the actor must be a character rather than perform as such.) The actor knows that if he says his lines in a competent manner he will avoid trouble. Since the director may not be aware of the actor's full potential, he will accept the performance as the actor's best. But is it?

The good director always encourages his actors to take chances, to try for something new, something beyond the accepted interpretation, and most of the truly gifted actors will try to surpass themselves if they are confident the director will not allow them to look foolish. The director should observe the actor's creative flights with a discriminating and analytical (but not critical) eye. He should separate the good from the bad and communicate his analysis to the actor, who will shade his efforts accordingly. The hoped-for result is that always welcome comment from the critics: "The player lived the part. She *was* Jane Doe."

On location in Paris, Montgomery Clift would sometimes awaken me at two or three in the morning with, "Come on up! I've got something to show you." (Thank God we were staying at the same hotel!) When I arrived in his room, he would demonstrate an idea for some future day's work, sometimes (even when sober) literally climbing the walls. I knew him well enough to know that that would not be his on-set performance, so I would try to understand what he was getting at, and I usually did. If I said, "Monty, I'm not too sure," his immediate response was always, "OK, let's forget it. We'll come up with something better." Although more often than not his idea was not what I wanted, when he did strike the right chord, it was a plus, an improvement on the original conception.

The point is that he felt secure enough with me to try anything, no matter how bizarre it might seem at the time. The bizarre, properly rescaled and rearranged, can become reality—an exciting, effective reality, the kind that surprises the audience but leaves it thinking, "That's it! That's just the way it is!" It is that kind of audience reaction that distinguishes every really fine film from the ordinary.

Of course, such cooperation between actor and director requires mutual confidence, and mutual confidence is based on open communication. There is always at least one little imp in paradise. People differ, communication is not always easy, some insecurities are very deep-seated. They will have nothing to do with scenes, scripts, or roles, but lie deeply buried in the personalities of the people involved. They have commonly, and and I think mistakenly, been lumped under the category of temperament. These insecurities are sometimes exceedingly difficult to deal with.

Webster's dictionary defines temperamental as "having or showing a sensitive, easily exited temperament." And temperament, in turn, is defined as "constitution or frame of mind; esp. the character of mind or of mental reactions characteristic of an individual."

Straightforward and, except for inclusion of the borderline words "easily excited," hardly pejorative. But the word temperamental as understood by the man in the street has come to have a decidedly derogatory meaning, and is used primarily as a criticism of performers—musicians, opera stars, and actors. Even top athletes who dare to bridle at stupid questions are branded as temperamental by the sports-writing community. Since temperament does exist and must occasionally be accommodated or dealt with, it will pay us to analyze this highly misunderstood word.

Fifty years ago Thomas Wolfe wrote, "The effort of . . . creating something seems to start up a . . . bewildering conflict in the man who does it . . . so that he feels he is struggling not only with his own work but also with the whole world around him, and he is so beset with . . . bewilderment that he lashes out at everyone . . . even against . . . his true friends."

The question arises, Why does the artist experience such conflicts? The chief cause is insecurity—not only concerning his creation, but concerning its acceptance by critics and audiences. The artist is always before the bar. He is forever being judged and he never knows in advance whether the verdict will be "success" or "failure."

Even success in one film gives him only temporary relief. While singing the creator's praises the critics will often hedge their bets with phrases like, "Now we must wait to see if the artist has more bullets in his gun, or if this is strictly a one-shot deal," leaving the creator to wonder if he will ever be able to live up to the things said about him and his work. The better the work, the sharper the reaction if his next effort fails in the slightest. In the interest of trying new ways the artist cries, "Give me the right to fail!" But the critics and the people usually turn a deaf ear.

Actors are, as they should be, extremely sensitive, and suffer in varying degrees from this syndrome. The older, more experienced artists will have come to terms with it. The younger or less analytical will strike out at the world around them—and on the set that usually means the director, who is by no means immune from attacks of insecurity himself. If he is sympathetic and supportive, he will try to make the troubled actor understand that although creation is a battle, it is a battle that must be fought within oneself. If he can get that message across, he will find that the bouts of temperament will steadily diminish.

Another problem of temperament stems from insecurity of the ego rather than of the creative urge. On rare occasions the director will face a test of strength with an actor, and not necessarily a star. The actor may just be trying the director to see if the latter has the strength to run the company. His own security and part of his career may depend on it. He is usually someone who has been around long enough to know that a weak director will probably produce a weak film. Once his doubts are removed and he is satisfied that the director can cut the mustard, the rest is easy sailing, at least in the area of personality conflict.

Occasionally, however, for ego-oriented reasons, an actor wants to be king of the hill. His challenge comes early and unmistakably. If the director is to remain in charge of the film, this is a battle he must win.

The challenges vary and so do the solutions, but it is vital that the director recognize the signs immediately and quickly arrive at the answer. Since this is a rather vague exposition, an example is in order. The following is a mild, almost amusing one, but it could have become quite serious. It occurred on one of my first films. I was young and inexperienced. A middle-aged actor, a man of talent and himself a long-time director of little-theater productions, was playing an important role. From the beginning, he would approach me early in the day. The dialogue would run something like this:

"Eddie, I've been going over today's scene, and I've got a few problems." (Of course, we had already worked out the scene the day before.)

"What bothers you?"

"Well, here where I say, 'thank you,' I'd be more comfortable with 'much obliged.' And here, where I have to say, 'good-bye,' I'd rather say, 'so long.' "

The lines were usually more complex than I have indicated, but his changes were that inconsequential. That was the crux of the matter. He was simply putting me on the spot, forcing me to defend the scene exactly as written, or give in to his piddling demands. It was the transference of decision-making authority that mattered, not the dialogue.

I resisted, of course, feeling rather foolish and uncomfortable. For two or three days I was in a quandary. Then I arrived at a solution. As he walked onto the set one morning I called him over to me. I had already had his chair placed beside mine.

"Sit down, John," I said.

"What's up?"

"I went over your scene again last night, and I have a few suggestions." He raised an eyebrow at me. "Here," I said, "where you say, 'I'd rather not,' I felt you might be more comfortable saying, 'I don't think I should.' " He looked at me for a long moment.

"No," he said. "I feel quite comfortable with the line as it is."

"Fine. But here, where you say, 'I'll be there tonight,' wouldn't you rather say, 'I'll be there this evening?' " Another long pause.

"Oh, I think 'I'll be there tonight' is satisfactory."

So it went throughout the scene, but he was now the uncomfortable one. I was not sure whether it was because I was now putting him under the gun, or just that he realized I was on to his game, but he never challenged me again. From then on he listened cooperatively to any suggestions I had to make.

This brings us around to style—the director's style. Each director has his own, but it is simply a variation of two basic techniques. The first, which is rapidly disappearing, is what was once called teutonic. The origin of the word and the technique is obvious. The early German directors who came to Hollywood were quite dictatorial. Dick Powell recounted an experience with one such.

"You walk through that door," he told Powell, "take four steps into the room, stop, count three, then look to your right."

This *important* scene from Crossfire *was called daring by some because it ran for so long without dialogue. Dmytryk let the two actors, Gloria Graham and George Cooper, tell the story with their emotions and actions rather than words.*

"Why?", asked Powell.

"Because I tell you to," was the answer. Throughout the rather uncomfortable film, it was the only answer he got.

Today it would be unthinkable for the director not to discuss a scene with his actors. Even if the director is quite adamant about a particular treatment, there should be a complete understanding of what the moves are and why. He might even explain his setups and what effects he hopes they will achieve. Then he will encourage the actors to fit their established characterizations into the desired pattern and to integrate their concepts with his. If the director's treatment is valid, there will be no difficulty in giving him everything he is looking for, and more.

The teutonic method may still be useful, but only for a highly stylized film. Certain so-called art films may depend on exact juxtaposition of setup and scene, but even then there is probably more to be gained by making an actor aware of the desired result. Who knows? He may even be able to contribute a little.

It may relieve the reader to learn that almost everything I say in this book has its exceptions. Here, I must register an especially marked one, where the exception is, thank goodness, the rule. On rereading this chapter I have realized I may be, to put it gently, scaring the daylights out of the potential young director. To put his mind at ease, I hasten to say that the troublesome actor is rare. I have never had more than one or two in any one film, and the casts of most of my films were 100 percent talented, pleasant, and a joy to work with. The true professionals like Tracy, Bogart, E. G. Marshall, Agnes Moorehead, Deborah Kerr, Van Johnson, and many, many others were magic, and working with them almost canceled out the tribulations of producers, finances, and logistics. But even one carelessly tossed monkey wrench can create havoc in an otherwise perfectly running machine, and it behooves the aspiring director to recognize personality problems and to learn how to deal with them.

The matters of insecurity and the tender ego have been discussed at some length, as has the need for bolstering them. There are a number of ways of accomplishing this. To aid the uninitiated, let me mention a few.

First, it pays to praise a job well done on every possible occasion. This also applies to the crew. Second, full and open credit should be given to anyone making a useful suggestion.

It can be stated as an axiom that the greater one's insecurity, the more vulnerable is one's sense of dignity. So, third, any statement or action that is belittling must be avoided, especially on an open set. A world-champion boxer will shrug off a drunken challenge to his manhood, but an insecure actor will react strongly to a tactless questioning of his talent. I have seen a good character actor destroyed by a cruel and thoughtless director who was engaged in his own struggle with the world around him. A director who openly criticizes actors in front of the crew and fellow artists is certain to make the objects of his scorn withdraw into themselves. How, then, can he expect to get an outgoing and natural performance? The director who neglects to treat an actor as his equal is doing himself a great disservice. If not for the sake of decency, then surely for the sake of the film and his own reputation he should behave in a manner that will guarantee the actor's wholehearted support.

During the first rehearsal of any scene there will inevitably be mistakes—in timing, movement, or dialogue. It is counterproductive to enumerate, or even mention, such mistakes until more rehearsals have taken place, and then it will probably be unnecessary. The actor is surely aware of his miscues and, like most of us, he hates to have them brought to his attention. Given time, he will work out the problems until he has the proper treatment down pat. Making him aware of his errors too early in the going not only violates his sense of dignity, but may create a block in his mind that can cause difficulties in succeeding rehearsals or takes.

If, as sometimes happens, the actor is unaware of a mistake and persists in it, the wise course of action is to take him aside and clarify the problem quietly and privately. The actor will appreciate this, and his confidence in the director will increase accordingly.*

At other times an actor may misread a line, not out of ignorance but because his conception of its meaning may not be the desired one; it happens to the best of them. A correction must be made, but how? Obviously, the actor can read a line better

---

*Of course, not all corrections are made in so prudent a manner. In the give and take of an enthusiastic rehearsal, suggestions are sometimes broadcast for the entire set to hear.

than I can, or he would not be in my film. Laurence Olivier aside, how many directors can tell Paul Newman or Dustin Hoffman how to speak effectively? Certainly not I, even though I should know what is right or what is wrong when I hear it. Only in extreme cases will I give an actor what I consider a proper reading. Instead, in casual conversation I will recount an experience or tell a funny story that somehow illustrates the proper meaning of the misread line. No matter how subtle I try to be, I am always surprised at how quickly the actor will say "Gotcha!" The next time the scene is played the reading will be perfect.

Anything that makes the actor conscious of the set-world around him while shooting detracts from his concentration. Consequently, the camera crew and the dialogue director should be instructed never to speak directly to an actor about "hitting his marks" or matching his action unless he specifically asks for such information. The same holds true for the sound mixer; if he has trouble hearing a line he should, like the cameraman or the script clerk, check with the director, who will discuss the problem with the actor at the propitious time.

The player's "eye line," that is, the area his eyes may look out on during the playing of a scene, should also be kept clear, both of visitors and of members of the crew; some movement, however far in the background, may catch his attention and distract him.

It is very important to keep one other stricture in mind. On the set, the actor must rely only on the director for correction, assistance, or approval. If he is in any doubt about where he should look when the director says "cut!", he, the director, and the film are in serious trouble.

Since the primary focus of this chapter has been on psychological traits and attitudes, one further bit of information is in order. Aside from, or possibly because of, all the miseries that accompany the making of a difficult film—the irritable stomach, the occupational nightmares, the nocturnal shakes—if the schedule runs more than forty days, paranoia is sure to raise its ugly head. The creative people start feeling sorry for themselves and suspicion toward each other. Each one is certain all the others are ganging up to do him in.

Only one thing can be done about it; recognize it for what it is, a temporary aberration of perception. The act of recognition serves to defuse its more dangerous effects. Beyond that, I recommend that the director pretend he is observing his little world of filmmaking from far beyond the stratosphere. He will be amazed how small his problems will look from that perspective.

When actors are on camera for close-ups, Dmytryk insists that
the other actors in the group be on stage, and not be represented
by stand-ins. Here Robert Young is filmed close up for Crossfire
with Robert Mitchum throwing his lines to Young.

7

Shooting Techniques

Critics and students of films often say, "Movies are a director's medium." That is hardly an arguable conclusion, but what exactly is it that makes the statement true?

The making of a motion picture can be roughly divided into four categories—story, interpretation (acting), editing, and shooting techniques. The director has a good deal of input in all of these areas, but his control over the last category is total. Unless he has a thorough knowledge of film staging and setups, his films will always be found wanting, regardless of the quality of the other three basic elements.

The director does not simply stage a scene, point the camera at it, and record it on film. Nor, if he wants to be regarded as a master of his craft, does he limit himself to routine long shots, group shots, two-shots, and close-ups. There is an almost infinite number of variations of these primitive classifications, and the director should have such a close acquaintance with all of them that he can bring them into use instinctively. He should not have to labor, as I have seen some inexpert directors do, to solve a simple setup problem.

Experience can sometimes be a millstone around the director's neck, however. After years of using most of the setups in the book, the temptation to fall back on a dependable technique is very strong. If the director has a solid conception of his physical treatment of the scene, his positioning of the camera—the setup—

will be automatic, or almost so. He should at all times search his mind for a variation that will enable him to present the scene at its best. Much will depend on its place in the film and on its intensity. A setup that might work perfectly near the start of the film may fall short if it is used for a similar grouping at or near the climax.

Although a thorough knowledge of these mechanics is of prime concern, the director's creative instinct is his most important asset. Only on it can he build a reputation for style and film-making excellence. Nuances are as important in a setup as they are in a line of dialogue or in a performance, but if the audience sees them as such the director has failed. Like properly used symbols, nuances should enrich the scene as a whole, and not be seen as an exercise in theory or technique. A director's touch should be recognized only in postviewing analysis.

Ordinarily, a setup cannot be selected until the director knows how the scene is going to play. Unless he is a disciple of the teutonic school, he will not know that precisely until he has had a run-through or rehearsal.

Ever since the invasion of sound into films there has been some argument about the relative merits of full theatrical style pre-production rehearsals versus pre-scene rehearsals held immediately prior to shooting. Both methods have been used, but the overwhelming percentage of filmmakers employ the latter. Full rehearsals were originally favored by the directors who came to films by way of the theater. It was the technique with which they were familiar and, more important perhaps, it gave them the opportunity to see the eventual actuality in the embryo. The director who has been trained primarily in filmmaking has learned to visualize the whole film while familiarizing himself with the script. Although his general conception is formed at that time, he has the added advantage of keeping himself loose for possible changes he will make as shooting progresses and the film comes to life. The full rehearsal too often sets the form of the film; when actual production starts, the mind resists further changes, especially when filming falls behind schedule and the going gets tough.

An additional problem with pre-production rehearsals is that the full cast is rarely available. Since a player must be paid from the day he reports for work (and rehearsal is work), the expense of hiring actors who may not be used until late in the schedule becomes a factor.

A marked advantage of the pre-scene rehearsal is that the actors need only memorize that scene's dialogue. For all but those few who have a photographic memory, this is a convenience that is greatly appreciated.

A method of working that has served me remarkably well is to rehearse a scene the day before it is to be shot. The current day's filming comes to a halt about 4:30 in the afternoon. The stage is cleared of all except key personnel and, with the next day's cast on the set, a casual reading is held to get the feel of the scene. The next step is to work out the moves in conjunction with the dialogue.* The rehearsal may require as little as twenty minutes or as much as an hour and a half, and when it is finished the next morning's first setup is laid out. Now cast and crew can leave the studio knowing what is expected of them on the following day. Dialogue and movement problems have been discussed and solved, every actor knows what to expect from the director and from the rest of the cast, the cameraman knows his lighting requirements, the gaffer and the prop man are aware of any new equipment or props that may be needed, and the assistant can place his calls with accuracy. All, including the director, can go home feeling that tomorrow's work is "in the bag."

The early "wrap" has many collateral advantages. The film's creative minds are still relatively fresh, and that is an important consideration. An eight-hour day is tiring, both physically and mentally, especially after the first few weeks. The juices dry up and ideas germinate reluctantly. Both cast and crew are more inclined to settle for the routine. Fatigue shows in the actors' eyes; even the make-up cracks, and a patch-up job is always a patch-up job.

Strange as it may seem, this short day method of working has always saved me a good deal of time. Every film made in this fashion was brought in under schedule and under budget. Benefits to the films were incalculable.

Early filmmakers customarily started each new sequence with what is called an establishing shot. As the name implies, this is

*A more explicit exposition of the rehearsal routine is contained in Chapter 9.

Sometimes there is no question that a scene will go unrehearsed, and that the first take will be the only one. In this scene from The Mountain, *Robert Wagner runs down a virgin snowfield with a bag of loot.*

a setup that shows the characters in their milieu, whether it be an interior of a building or a spot on location. Before it is broken up into closer setups, the entire scene is often played in the establishing shot, even though only a relatively short portion of the take is intended for use in the edited film. It was also a rule that there be a progression from longer to closer setups in cutting the scene. Although a few of today's directors still follow this rule, it is usually ignored by the more creative filmmakers. If the achieved effect is dramatically sound, one can cut from a long shot into an extreme close-up, or vice versa. In one film I made a point of starting each new sequence with a close shot, disclosing the background only as the actors moved through it. Even though I made no effort to show the audience the setting of any of the scenes, the review in *Time* magazine commented particularly on the effective design and use of sets.

I have found the establishing shot a waste of time and money except in one specific instance. If I am not quite sure of a scene or a planned setup, I will shoot such a shot. It allows me to observe the scene as a whole and to pinpoint doubtful areas, and it gives me time to gather my thoughts and work out the necessary corrections or setups. On a more realistic level, the production report gives me credit for shooting rather than thinking, which, at the daily production running impresses those executives who believe that thinking is an unnecessary expenditure of set time.

None of this is meant to imply that a long shot is a useless setup. On the contrary, its intelligent use, as beautifully demonstrated in *The Black Stallion*, can be a tremendous asset. But too often, especially in TV films, it is resorted to solely as an establishing shot. As such, it is doing only half its job. Every shot, when properly used, should advance the dramatic thrust of the story.

If the director is filming a football game, for instance, he might choose to start his sequence with a long shot of the stadium rather than a close shot of the team huddle. This serves to establish that there is a football game in progress with a large crowd in attendance, nothing more. Now, think of the sequence as starting in a different way; a close shot of the quarterback barking signals; then, in a series of cuts, the center hands him the ball, the play develops, the receiver streaks down the field, the quarterback evades a tackler and releases the ball, and the receiver catches it in the end zone. Now, for the first time, there is a full shot of the stadium as the crowd rises to its feet screaming. The long shot here is employed for dramatic emphasis, as well as an establishing shot. Even though the background is exposed incidentally, at no point would an audience doubt that the game was being played on the gridiron.

Positioning the camera for a setup is the prerogative of the director, not the cameraman. Only the director knows what he wants the camera to see—what he wants to include in the frame and, just as important, what he wants to exclude.

There are two methods for lining up a shot. The first is to establish the setup, then stage the scene within the area the setup covers. I call this "bringing the actors to the camera." The second is to work out the movements with the actors, then position the camera to pick up the rehearsed action in the most effective way. This I call "bringing the camera to the actors." Both methods are useful, though for most scenes I prefer the second. The actors have greater freedom for being. There is no artificial constraint, although careless wandering, which will occasionally occur, especially with some method actors, should be resisted.

The first procedure is useful in scenes where visual effects are of prime importance or in shots where the background plays a vital role. In general, the method that allows the actor the freedom he needs to help improve the development of his character is the most desirable. In truth, many of my setups are the result of the combination of the two; I allow the actors full freedom until they feel comfortable. Then, as rehearsals progress, I tighten the moves and particularize the positions until the staging is most camera-effective. By that time both the cast and I are ready to shoot.

A setup that lends the scene a dynamic quality is obviously to be preferred to a stodgy snapshot. Here, staging and setup go hand in hand. But to confine ourselves strictly to the setup at this point, there are a few important observations to be made.

The dullest possible shot is one made at eye level. It adds absolutely nothing new to the picture. Unless one is Wilt Chamberlain or a Munchkin, it is the everyday point of view of every person over the age of sixteen. It is preferable to position the lens either somewhat below or somewhat above eye level. The variation from normal should not be too obvious, but it should be offbeat enough to give the viewer a subconscious nudge. The choice of above or below the level of the eye will depend upon the nature of the shot. Normally, the low setup is preferable for close group shots or close-ups. One advantage of this position is that it affords a better look at the actor's eyes; in a high-level shot the viewer would be looking down at the player's eyelids.

The high setup is especially useful for long shots or full shots in cramped areas. In most long shots it is preferable to see the ground on which the actors stand rather than yards of empty space over their heads. The fuller the shot, the higher the lens can go. It must be reemphasized that there are exceptions to these generalizations, even in respect to the eye-level shot, which can, of course, be useful. But when an exception is made, it should be for a very positive reason.

What has been said for the eye-level shot can be repeated for the profile shot. Outside of a better view of the ears, little can be gained from such a positioning. The eyes are not clearly visible, depriving the film of one of its great advantages, and the figures (usually two) are of similar size, depriving the audience of the dynamic effect of size differential. *

As previously stated, the actor's eyes are unquestionably his most effective means for transmitting emotion. In *Wuthering Heights*, the eyes in any one of Laurence Olivier's close-ups expressed more love than all the writhing bodies in the films of the last decade. By the honest use of his eyes a fine actor can register almost any emotion without "making a face." It is worthwhile to repeat that "The eyes are the windows of the soul."

The shoddy way the close-up has been misused and overused by the great majority of TV directors has done this special shot a great disservice. Like any valuable technique, the close-up should not be used indiscriminately lest it lose its value. At its best, it is climactic, and it should be reserved for climactic moments. Every editor knows that the simple act of cutting from a general shot to a close-up adds an important dimension or significance to any scene. But the continual use of close-ups leaves him nothing to pull out of the bag.

---

*An obvious exception is a shot made against the setting sun. The resulting silhouettes project a beautiful effect of their own.

The scope of the setup is determined by the amount of information the shot should deliver and the dramatic impact the director wants to make. In his Westerns, John Ford took advantage of his backgrounds. To do this he used the startling scenery of locations like Monument Valley and well-placed camera setups. The impact of the beauty, the starkness, and the loneliness of his long shots added greatly to the viewers' understanding and appreciation of the characters inhabiting those areas. As the opposite end of the scale, Hitchcock used extreme close-ups superbly to instill fear and terror as his characters reacted to startling or inhuman confrontations.

In short, each setup should say exactly what the director wants it to say. If it discloses less than he desires, the hoped-for effect on the audience is diminished. If it gives more information than necessary, it dirties up the scene and confuses the audience. No matter how artistic the setup might be, if the audience is confused it is also bored.

Incidentally, in speaking of close-ups one speaks of a variety of shots. A close-up can be an individual, that is, a waist figure of one person, or it can creep increasingly closer to the player until, at the other extreme, only two eyes are seen. Such a shot is used only for an intensely emotional reaction.

The lighting of a close-up can vary considerably from the lighting of the general scene. Like the choice of size, it depends on the dramatic emphasis and the immediate mood required. It can be beautifully shaded, shot against the set background or against a portrait flat. When it is properly integrated into the edited sequence, not a soul will notice any difference in treatment. Whatever the lighting style, one thing should be remembered— the eye light. This is a specially adjusted light source that appears as a small highlight in each of the actor's eyes and makes them come alive. The proper use of this technique is rapidly disappearing as flat TV lighting takes over, but it is most important and should always be used unless, of course, an appearance of dullness is desired.

In staging a setup for more than one person, grouping is a prime consideration. It is essential that the camera should record only what the audience should see. What is left out of the shot can be as important as what is kept in. Many years ago I watched the shooting of a small group scene. The people involved were a young husband and wife and the wife's parents. The director was one of several theatrical directors remaining in Hollywood after the exodus of most of those who earlier invaded the town with the coming of sound. Quite naturally, his techniques had been learned in the theater, and he had never made a complete adjustment to the special demands of the screen.

In the scene, the parents started a somewhat bitter argument with the young couple. Shortly after the start of the scene the mother took over for both herself and her husband. At this point, the director had the father move off to the side of the room, where he proceeded to scan the titles of books on a shelf, leaving the other three to continue the argument in front of the camera. Later, I asked the director why he had asked the father to leave the scene, the last thing a truly concerned parent would have done.

"I wanted him out of the shot," he answered. "He was standing out like a sore thumb."

I did not mention that a film director would simply have moved his camera up to a three-shot, thus eliminating what he considered an awkward grouping. As a matter of fact, an individual shot of the father would then have served as a useful cut, showing his reaction to pertinent parts of the conversation in which he was vitally interested, even though he was not a verbal participant. The shot would also have served as a protection cut if the master scene had had to be shortened.

In another instance, a tyro director told me. "I've finally learned the secret of staging for the screen. I just visualize the action as though it were taking place under the proscenium." The few films he made looked it. The viewer was always looking at a scene, an illustration with a neat border around it, rather than being *in* the scene, participating with the characters on the screen. Whenever possible, which is most of the time, I get in as tight as the grouping will allow. The shoulders of the characters on either side of the shot should be out of the frame, giving the viewer a participant's perception. This technique of having someone or something in the picture extend outside the edges of the frame is quite important. Even in extra-long shots, where the actors are near the center of the screen, a foreground piece of some sort—a stick of furniture in an interior, a rock or a shrub in a country location, a trash can on a busy street—cutting in on the edge of the frame will serve to enhance the impression of linear continuity between the viewer and the image. When properly lit and integrated into the rest of the picture, foreground pieces add significantly to the illusion of a third dimension.

There is a kindergarten fault in staging that is inexcusable. I refer to lining up the actors. It may be acceptable in a sitcom, but never in a film. Yet I have seen experienced directors align their people as if they were standing inspection. Except in rare circumstances, people in real life do not stand side by side to hold a conversation. They are usually face to face, whether there are two, three, or more participants.

Here I want to reiterate: Film actors are not on the stage. There is no upstage or downstage on the film set. There is no fixed directional relationship to an audience, real or imaginary. Actors do not play within the confines of a narrow sector; theirs is a 360-degree world, just as it is in real life. It should come as no surprise that the camera can move anywhere within the full circle. If an actor feels slighted because his back is to the camera in a group shot, a reverse close shot will quickly put his nose back in joint.

That is the real secret of proper staging. No matter where or how an actor stands in one shot, he can be presented from a different perspective in another. If the director understands cutting even slightly, he can properly design setups to cover any grouping.

Another useful consequence of the camera's freedom of movement is known simply as "cheating." A filmmaker cheats in many ways—with make-up, with lenses and lens filters, with lighting—but the word cheating is reserved for a special technique that might be called arbitrary positional variation. That means that as setups are changed, the positions of the actors relative to each other or to their setting can also be changed. If understood, this may seem obvious, but many directors become completely confused when confronted by the need arbitrarily to change positions. Before things get out of hand two simple examples should clarify the concept for the beginner.

Example one: A scene involving two people. The background for the action is a desert location featuring cactus and Joshua trees. The scene is four or five pages in length and will require a full day to shoot.

Location filming always starts as early in the morning as possible, the actual time depending on the season of the year. The light is good either early in the morning or rather late in the afternoon. High noon brings flat light and an unattractive picture. In the morning, the sun lies to the east, casting, let us say, shadows on the left side of the lead actor's face. In the late afternoon, the sun lies to the west and, if the actors maintain their original positions relative to the background, the shadows will be on the right side of the actor's face. If we shoot a medium shot early in the morning and a close shot covering the same action later in the afternoon, the shadows will jump from one side of the face to the other with every cut, at least if the actors retain their original positions.

The solution: Move the actors in a half circle on the ground even as the sun sails in its arc across the sky, thus keeping the facial shadows relatively consistent. The background will change but, unless it is of more importance to the scene than the foreground action, no one will notice it, not even the next day in the rushes.

Example two: A small group in a room—say, a home library—lit in a subdued fashion. A door in the background opens onto a brightly lit living room where a party is in progress. In the full shot, the background as a whole is shadowed, but when the camera is lined up for a close shot of one of the actors in the group, it is found that he is framed against the brightly lit door, which now dominates the picture. To cut from the subdued scene to the brightly lit one would deliver an undesirable shock. Solution: Arbitrarily move the actor to a more suitable background. Again, if properly shot and cut, it will not be noticeable.

Such cheating is frequently resorted to, sometimes in an extremely sophisticated and complex manner. But for that the director needs a good deal of experience, and an almost mathematical sense of positional relativity.

Whether the camera simply pans the actor across a set or moves with him on a dolly track, the moving shot has much the same requirements as the stationary shot, except for one thing—the start. An obvious start to a camera movement will often make the viewer conscious of the mechanics and pull him back into the theater. To circumvent this, many ploys are available. The simplest is to have the actor move first. Once the viewer's eye starts to follow the actor across the screen, the panning of the camera will appear to be a natural extension of his movement. To move away from a static composition is more difficult.

An example: The director wants to pull back from a pile of trash at the entrance to an alley, then pan to a full shot of the street. A simple stratagem would be to have a slight breeze (stirred up by a fan, if necessary) blow a piece of paper out of the trash pile in the direction of the camera pan. As the scrap of paper flies through the air, the camera moves with it, panning and pulling back simultaneously. Once the action is properly started, the rest of the movement is acceptable on its own.

Another example: A close shot of an ash tray on a table, holding a burning cigarette. A hand reaches in and picks up the cigarette. As the hand withdraws, the camera moves with it, disclosing first, the owner of the hand and eventually, a room full of people. The two examples, for easy understanding, are clichés. They can be taken from there; all one needs is a little imagination.

There is another kind of camera movement that is even more commonly used. It is what might be called a corrective move. Except for extreme long shots and tight close-ups, the camera should rarely be fixed throughout the scene. If one of the actors makes a move, a compositional adjustment may be required and the camera must move to accommodate it. (I do not speak here of a simple correction made by moving the camera head, but one made by moving the entire camera on a dolly. For most shots, a crab dolly is a necessity.) The movement can be as short as six inches or as long as several feet. It is the only way to maintain an attractive composition while keeping the scene fluid.

So far we have been discussing limited groupings, but crowds are also an element in many films. The crowd shot is the bete noire of many a director, most of whom are mild agoraphobics to begin with, and it motivates some of them to delegate the handling of background crowds to the assistant. This shifts the responsibility, but hardly solves the problem.

The film crowd is difficult to deal with on a creative level because it has no entity of its own. It is just a crowd, a horde of nameless, featureless extras, muttering unintelligible phrases and engaged in meaningless activity. One solution is to make the crowd a mob; a mob always has a purpose. The earlier example of the football crowd is appropriate. If we start with the crowd, we have only a large number of people gathered in a stadium. If we reserve a view of the stadium until the touchdown is made, we show a large number of individuals in a mob response to the exciting action on the field. The crowd now has a common purpose and a common reaction.

When no common purpose is possible, as in a party sequence, it is wise to break the crowd up into its components—first, into manageable groups, then into individuals. Each individual is given a background and a purpose. Then the process is reversed; the individuals become a part of a group, and the groups merge into a crowd. For the actual shooting it is preferable to follow one person, someone whom we know or want to know, through the crowd. Starting with a close shot of our actor, and always keeping him as the center of interest, we pull back as he moves through the room to discover the presence of the crowd.

In shooting an actor against a crowd background (say, at a race track) it is often useful to diminish the crowd concentration as the camera moves closer (in separate cuts) to the center of interest. In a tight close-up, the crowd can be eliminated entirely. The closer the camera comes to the actor, the more distracting the background people are. In the close-up, the viewer's attention should be concentrated on the actor. As in all good cheating, what is not on the screen will hardly be missed.

Dmytryk, flanked by camerman Gabor Pogany, sets up a scene for Bluebeard.

8

Use of Lenses

Recently, a master's degree candidate was reading his prethesis paper to a board of examiners. His subject was the genre known as film noire. In some detail, he mentioned social ramifications, lighting treatment, and a few other pertinent factors, but at no time did he mention the selective use of lenses, without which film noire could hardly exist.

Most people have some acquaintance with still cameras, and they know that lenses have different focal lengths, which they classify broadly as normal, close-up, and telephoto. The film student knows that the 35mm film camera uses a number of lenses of specific focal lengths. He *should* know that each lens has specific uses.

The normal lens complement for a 35mm camera would be one of each of the following: 25mm, 35mm, 50mm, 75mm, 100mm, and possibly a zoom lens. Zoom lenses, although very popular in the 16mm field, are little used in professional filmmaking except for special moving-in and telescopic shots.*Zoom lenses, too, have varying limits of magnification.

The 50mm is the standard, or normal, lens in filmmaking. That means that a figure shot at a distance of twenty feet from the camera will appear to be twenty feet from the viewer when

---

*For reasons having to do with background distortion, whenever possible a moving-in shot is made with a dolly and a lens of fixed focal length.

he sees it on the screen. The background will also appear to be quite normal, as will the lines of perspective.

Any lens with a focal length below 50mm is called a wide-angle lens. Like all lenses outside of normal range, wide-angle lenses have special properties that are actually distortions from the normal. For example, a 25mm lens will make a figure standing twenty feet from the camera appear to be forty feet away when seen on the screen. Each succeeding plane behind the figure will also have doubled its apparent distance from the viewer. A fountain, say, that is actually 100 feet behind the figure will now appear to be 240 feet away. (A 35mm lens will make the same figure appear to be about 32 feet from the camera and the background would recede to an apparent distance of about 160 feet.) Such lenses not only artificially lengthen the distance between object and viewer they broaden the background proportionately; hence the term wide-angle. It is the first property that has the greatest application in films, however.

The narrow-angle lenses, as the term implies, impart an opposite effect; they narrow the width of the background and diminish the apparent distance between the object and the viewer. If shot with a 100mm lens, the figure at twenty feet will now appear to be ten feet from the camera. Longer focal-length lenses are increasingly telescopic.

All this is basic knowledge to the camera buff and the cameraman, but what does it mean to the average director? Unfortunately, not much. But it should mean a great deal, as a few examples will show.

An actor, starting at a distance of twenty feet, will take eight steps to reach the camera. When photographed with a 50mm lens, the action on the screen will appear to be quite normal— and quite ordinary. If the same action from the same distance is now shot with a 25mm lens it will take the actor the same eight steps to reach the camera. As seen on the screen, however, he will appear to be approaching from forty feet away. In other words, taking the same number of steps and moving at the same pace and with the same effort, he will apparently cover twice the distance of the first shot. Each stride will now appear to be five feet long instead of the normal thirty inches. Interesting, but what is the practical application?

Let us say we are filming a modern version of *Dr. Jekyll and*

Mr. Hyde. Whenever Dr. Jekyll is before the camera we will use a 50mm lens, showing him as an ordinary human being with ordinary physical characteristics. When shooting the same actor as Mr. Hyde, we will use a 25mm lens. Immediately his movements will appear to be effortlessly greater, projecting a sense of superhuman power. Further distortion properties of the lens, which we will discuss shortly, will add to the appearance of menace.

A related effect can be obtained by moving the camera. Let us say we are shooting across a bed toward a door in the background, some twenty feet away. On the bed lies Mrs. Jekyll. In an early scene, the Doctor walks into the room to bid her goodnight. It takes him eight steps to reach the bedside. Later in the film, Hyde repeats the entrance of the earlier scene. But now we move the bed up to within ten feet of the door, and the camera is moved in proportionately. Since we are now using the 25mm lens, the door will still appear to be twenty feet in the background, but Hyde, like a vampire swooping down on his victim, can reach the bed in four steps. Miraculous? No, just clever use of the camera lens.

At the other end of the scale, if I wanted to show a man grow weak, I would shoot him with a 75 or even a 100mm lens. Then, since he would appear to be starting from a distance much closer than the actual twenty feet, each of his steps would seem to be short, weak, and ineffectual.

The instances here have purposely been caricatures, but a truly fine example of creative lens use appeared in a short, made some years ago, of Ambrose Bierce's *An Occurrence at Owl Creek Bridge.* Most of the film depicts a subconscious hallucinating experience. Near the climax, the lead actor is running desperately toward the safety of his home, but something in the real world is holding him back. He runs with all his strength but, as in a nightmare, he seems to make almost no progress. The scene was shot with a telescopic lens, which foreshortened his strides to inches instead of feet.

The same effect can be observed in scenes of racing horses shot from directly in front of the animals. Since the camera must be a great distance away to avoid collision, a telescopic, or narrow-angle, lens is used. The straining thoroughbreds, which actually take strides some twenty feet in length, seem to be marking time.

Because of the accompanying shallowness in depth, the horses also appear to be closely bunched, whereas a side angle would show them to be spread out over a considerable stretch of track.

This demonstrates another important property of the lens. The narrow-angle lens constricts the background and pulls it toward the camera, like the closed bellows of an accordian. The wide-angle lens, like the same bellows pulled out, expands the background. The degree of these effects in inversely proportional to the focal length of the lens used. The longer the focal length, the closer the image; the shorter the focal length, the deeper the background.

Used in conjunction with foreground pieces (see Chapter 7) and a properly lit scene, the wide-angle lens provides a much greater illusion of depth, or third dimension, than the normal lens. It also allows for a much deeper field of focus, which is often useful. Finally, this lens is a more efficient gatherer of light.

These properties offer opportunities for interesting effects. In *Christ in Concrete,* a woman lies in an old-fashioned brass bed, suffering the pangs of childbirth. The camera shoots over the back of her head toward her husband, who stands at the foot of the bed sharing her agony. During one spasm of pain, the woman grasps the bedpost behind her head, straining to stifle a scream. I wanted to show clearly the wedding ring on her clenched hand, while focusing sharply on her husband's face, some eight feet away. Since the camera was only a couple of feet behind the bed, carrying this depth of focus was extremely difficult. To solve the problem, we used a 25mm lens and doubled the amount of light. A normal lens would have rendered the shot impossible.

There are occasions, however, when deep, sharp focus is to be avoided, especially when a sense of depth are desired. Many film-makers have gone overboard for sharp background focus, but this only serves to flatten the picture. One of the necessary elements of depth perception is the relative sharpness of objects at different depths. A series of mountain ridges is optically separated from each other by subtle variations in color and softness of outline, which gives the distant view not only depth but beauty. If we focus at a beer mug held at arm's length, the background swims completely out of focus.

We take advantage of this effect when photographing most women in close-up. Such shots are usually made with a narrow-angle lens, generally the 75mm, which has the property of deemphasizing sharpness of feature by slightly flattening the face. Also, since the depth of focus is shallow, this lens can be sharply focused on the eyes, leaving the area around the ears and the front of the nose slightly softer. This serves to direct the viewer's attention more completely to the actor's eyes, which as has been repeatedly pointed out, are of paramount importance. (Incidentally, the lens stop is also a factor in most of these techniques.)

Softness means beauty in more ways than one. An actor who must look younger than his years obviously should be photographed softly. Erasure of facial lines, however, can be achieved more satisfactorily through the use of filters, in conjunction with the 75mm lens. This is a common practice, especially with actresses whose fans demand that they retain eternal youth. When using a filter, however, the director must try to be consistent. The director of one film starring an aging actress used a filter on all of her close-ups. Since youthful beauty was not required of the leading man, his close-ups were unfiltered. The difference in camera treatment and, unfortunately, the reason behind it were blatantly obvious when the close-ups were intercut. An effect that would have passed completely unnoticed if both close-ups had been filtered became obvious because of the thoughtlessness of the director and the carelessness of the cameraman.

The proper lenses, lens filters, and lighting can be used to good effect in covering facial skin imperfections as well. Due to an unfortunate bout with small pox, one of the leading stars of the forties had a pockmarked face, but no one suspected it from her film appearances.

Opposite effects can be obtained with side lighting and wide-angle lenses. A flat, featureless face can be given lines, planes, and even an angularity, which can enhance the appearance considerably. On occasion, even an apparent flaw can be revealed to good effect. Van Johnson bore a marked scar on his forehead that had been disguised with make-up and filters for his romantic roles at M-G-M. For the role of the mutinying officer of the USS *Caine*, however, the scar was made to order. Sharp focus and side lighting brought it out strongly, adding character to his usually rounded features.

The properties of the wide-angle lens which give us interesting full shots have to be carefully controlled in close-ups. An actor's nose appears to be twice as long as it really is when shot in close-up with a 25mm lens. This can be quite effective when ugliness or a sense of menace is desired, as for a Mr. Hyde, but in most instances men's close-ups are shot with the 50mm lens. There will be occasions, however, when the 35mm or even the 25mm lens, will be the lens of choice.

In *Crossfire*, for example, Robert Ryan played a psychotic killer. This aspect of his character was developed gradually during the course of the film. In the early scenes, his close-ups were shot with a 50mm lens, but as the story progressed, the focal length of his close-up lenses was diminished, first to 40mm, then 35mm, and finally to 25mm. (Any lens below that would have produced a too obvious distortion.) When the 25mm lens was used, Ryan's face was also greased with cocoa butter. The shiny skin, with every pore clearly delineated, gave him a truly menacing appearance.

It should be apparent that most of the useful effects obtained from the wide-angle lens require back-to-front movement or vice versa. There is little useful distortion if the actor moves straight across the screen. This kind of movement joins the eye-level and profile shots as a technique to be avoided. Let me try to describe an effective movement as compared to a flat one.

Many philosophers have pointed out that life is growth and growth is movement. This is certainly true for life on the screen. A moving, changing image is alive; and unmoving image is inert, dead. That is why a straight cross-screen walk-through, where the image remains constant in size even though it moves across the screen, is relatively dull. When the image moves from the background to the foreground, even as it moves from one side of the screen to the other, it grows in size with each succeeding frame. This makes a more marked impression on the observer's visual sense.

If at the same time we use a wide-angle lens, say, 35mm, the apparent lengthening of the mover's steps gives him added vitality and infuses the scene with more dynamism. Now we can and should go one step further by using an offbeat setup. If we place the lens a foot or so below eye level, the camera will be forced to tilt up with the moving figure as it approaches, until, just before it passes the camera, it seems to tower over the viewer. We now have additional movement and a further accentuation

CF-8

Low key lighting was the important element in helping actor Robert Ryan play the bad guy in Crossfire.

of the figure itself to add to its growth and its impact on the screen.

In an extreme case, at a climactic moment in a chase, for example, when we want to obtain the most dynamic effect possible, as the actor walks or runs toward the camera we can add still one more movement. The camera can dolly, if only for a short distance, against the actor's line of movement. In this case, as the actor moves from left to right the camera should be dollying from right to left, panning right and tilting up at the same time. If the camera is in the hands of a skillful operator, the only movement noticed by the viewer will be that of the actor, but, on the subconscious or subliminal level, the camera's contributions will have made the scene far more dynamic than if it had been shot with a 50mm lens from a stationary eye-level position.

The reader will have noticed the frequent use of the word distortion when referring to various properties of lenses. Distortions do exist, but owing to certain negative characteristics of our two-dimensional medium, unless vulgar extremes are resorted to, they are never obvious to the viewer, nor should they be. Their values lie in their effect on the viewer's subconscious, and in their ability to help emphasize character, appearance, and emotion. The director who knows how to use the setup and the lens to maximum effect leaves the actor free to be the character rather than to try to act him.

Consider a villain, a heavy. Evil men are not too uncommon, yet men who think of themselves as evil are extremely rare. Almost without exception, everyone rationalizes or justifies his actions. The thief who believes the world owes him a living, the embezzler who steals to bolster his unappreciated ego, the drug peddler who feels he is dealing in vital services, the tycoon who behaves uncharitably toward his competitors and his employees on the ground that it is "only good business," or the killer who sees his action as just retribution—all consider themselves whole, nonvillainous human beings, and they should be played that way by the actor. But if he has to depend completely on his own resources to portray his character's less desirable qualities, he may have to act more than may be acceptable.

On the other hand, if the director can use all of the techniques at his disposal to visually impart the texture of evil to an errant character, the actor will be free to play the part as a real human being rather than as a caricature. This applies to all the characters in a film. One of the great advantages of the medium is that there are so many techniques which if properly and creatively used, can reach beyond each performer's own resources to make a film's inhabitants more dynamic and more dramatically effective, while still keeping them human and real. These techniques have only been hinted at here, but if the reader sees the tip, he may become more readily aware of the iceberg.

At this point some reader will think, "Okay, I can vary the height of the camera, use different lenses and lighting effects, and so on. But how far should I raise or lower the camera, how do I select the proper lens for the proper shot, and what light effect do I ask for?"

Sorry. There are no specific answers. Rarely do situations repeat themselves exactly, and an answer would depend on the particular mood and action at a particular point in the film. Lowering the camera is a function of taste, not precept. The important thing is to take a crack at it, to risk the big gamble rather than settle for the small sure thing. It is often better to be creatively "wrong" than to be technically right. Consider El Greco. Experts may criticize a purposely out-of-focus shot or an out-of-focus line of dialogue, but what really counts in any work of art is the total effect, not technical perfection.

Director Dmytryk carefully outlines what he wants for a scene in Murder, My Sweet. *Dick Powell and Claire Trevor listen intently.*

9

The Heart of the Matter

Getting it on Film

So far we have considered mainly organizational and technical aspects of filmmaking, which, though very important in setting mood, enhancing dramatic impact, and creating an atmosphere of acceptance, are not really matters of life or death. To a considerable extent they are the packaging that makes the gift more exciting and possibly more acceptable. But an empty box, no matter how attractively wrapped, will be a disappointment, whereas the gift itself has a value even if stripped of all extraneous ornamentation. Examples of this are seen on the screen every day—stylishly packaged productions that have no content are financial and critical disasters, while crudely produced and executed films with strong dramatic or exploitational material become box office bonanzas.*

The intention here is not to diminish the value of the preceding chapters, but to stress a basic truth; what counts most is the life projected on the screen. That life will be rich and absorbing only when it is the result of honest writing, fine acting, and skillful

---

*Rossellini's masterpiece, *Rome, Open City*, was shot on raw stock discarded by the U.S. Army Signal Corps as unusable. The photography was dreadful; the film was a classic.

staging, and the responsibility for extracting the maximum yields out of these requisites is in the hands and the mind of the director. Therefore his approach to his work, the obstinacy with which he attacks his innumerable problems, becomes the single most important element in the making of a film.

Once the shooting starts the director gets little rest. His mind is on his scenes and their related problems throughout his waking hours. He dreams about them during his sleep. As the work progresses and his mind and body tire, his dreams become nightmares and the temptation to say "That's good enough, let's get on with it" grows stronger with each passing day.

But when is anything "good enough?" The answer is, never. Good enough implies there is something better, and if that's true, it makes little sense to settle for less. But we are getting ahead of ourselves. Let us begin while we are fresh, eager, and optimistic. Let us start with the first rehearsal.

Whenever possible, rehearsals should be held on the day before the rehearsed material is to be filmed. The material will usually consist of an entire sequence, which may be scheduled for several days of shooting, but the greatest concentration will be on the scenes to be done during the following day.

The first step is a casual reading of the scene. By this time some of the cast will have learned or memorized their lines; others will still be referring to their scripts. All will probably need some prompting. A few directors take on this duty themselves, but I recommend that it be delegated to the dialogue director or the script clerk. The director should be free to concentrate his entire attention on the actors as they read their lines and on the lines they read.

This reading—or readings, really, since there will usually be a number of them—is indispensable for a number of reasons:

1. Each actor learns how every other actor is developing his character. This may result in some modification of his own concept.
2. The actors become aware of each other's work habits. It is at this point that danger signals arise, and here the director should start planning strategies to neutralize acting methods that might eventually cause serious fric-

tion (see Ford vs Brando, Chapter 3). Fortunately, this is not a common problem, but occasionally it does come up.

3. The director, too, discovers his cast's work habits and follows the development of the actors' concepts.

4. Watching closely and listening carefully, the director catches dialogue redundancies (if any), becomes aware of areas that may need improvement or deeper development, makes mental notes of possible deletions or transpositions of phrases, and, together with the actors, begins to get a real sense of those points in the scene that should be stressed and those to be "thrown away."

A rehearsal, in short, is the time for slogging, and most of the slogging takes place during the readings. It is at this time that the final writing or rewriting takes place. (Here let me repeat, it is as important to know when to leave well enough alone as it is when to change it. Occasionally, a writer will give a director a gem. He must treasure it. He must help his actors to give it their best, then stand back and enjoy it.)

Although some scripts are better than others, few are perfect and the director would be remiss if he made no attempt to correct a weakness exposed by the actors' efforts to bring a scene to life. Such corrections are frequently made by referring the scene back to the original, or to a follow-up, writer. Not all directors are competent script doctors.

Now to specifics: First the dialogue. Each actor should make his dialogue his own, that is, he should commit himself to a way of speaking that best fulfills his screen character. This will involve a choice between proper or colloquial speech, a selection of regional accent (if necessary), a decision on possible speech affectations or impediments, and so on. Such decisions are made in consultation with the director, who must do his best to be objective. Some shaping or modification of the actors' concepts may be desirable, but any attempt by the director to superimpose his own ideas in this area can lead to boring similarities in characterization.

One director of the thirties had come to film from vaudeville, where he had performed a one-man act that consisted of playing ten different characters by donning ten different hats. That was exactly how he directed, figuratively putting one of his hats on each actor in his films. Needless to say, it showed.

Of course, not all roles require accents, affectations, or unusual ways of speaking. Most of them, in fact, are played by actors who superimpose their own personal speech patterns and mannerisms onto the imagined ones of the characters they are portraying. A healthy variety of characterizations can still be obtained, however, by permitting each actor a good deal of freedom in establishing his screen persona.

As mentioned previously, one of the most difficult and least well realized aspects of writing is good dialogue. It is essential that every line in a film (unless it is obviously a quotation) should appear to be spontaneous, but most lines have been written, re-written, honed, and polished until they sound anything but spontaneous. The most skillful actors have their own techniques for handling awkward or stilted lines, but such artists are as rare as great dialogue specialists. This anecdote may serve as an example.

While preparing a scene for a film with Spencer Tracy, I found one speech, some half-page in length, to be altogether too literary. I discussed the speech with Tracy and indicated that I was rewriting it in an attempt to bring it down to earth.

"I've already learned it," he told me. "Let's wait and see how it plays. If it proves awkward, we'll do your version."

We shot the scene the next day. While he played it, Tracy hemmed, hawed, hesitated, made slight repetitions. He broke it up so adroitly that it sounded completely extemporaneous. Perfect! But Tracy was probably the most skillful phraser in motion picture history. In most situations the director must be prepared to help his actors as they search for effective spontaneity.

In trying to achieve reality, some actors and directors resort to improvisation and students often enquire as to its worth. In the hands of a director with great editing skills, improvisation has some value but, unless one is to believe that actors can write better than skilled dramatists, it is wiser to cast a wary eye on this particular technique. If a scene proves to be especially stubborn, improvisation may furnish clues to the difficulties, as well as suggestions for possible solutions. The final version is then usually formalized by a writer or the director.

Another common source of trouble is the concept held by

many writers, directors, and especially actors, that every line of dialogue is important. It just is not so. As a matter of fact, I believe that half the lines in a well-written script are fillers or, in the language of the trade, throwaways. Back to Tracy again. He had a reputation for underplaying. In reality, he was only giving his lines the importance he felt they deserved, tossing them away. As he once said, "When a line is worth shouting, I can yell with the loudest of them." Indeed he could. To give a casual line the same weight and consideration as a crucial one is to overact. Most hamming consists of just that: making an offhand "Good evening" sound as earthshaking as a declaration of war.

In almost every film the most common problem is length—usually too much of it. Although overall length is given careful consideration from the moment of first writing, rehearsal readings will often reveal further redundancies in content as well as in phrasing. Such redundancies must be conscientiously eliminated.

The problem is often intensified by the director's inability to see the forest for the trees. Let us suppose that a desired dramatic effect depends on spreading the delivery of a particular piece of information over a number of scenes. In such a case, too definitive an exposition in any one sequence would destroy the desired effect by making further reference unnecessary. Therefore, if staggered information is important, the amount delivered in each scene must be pared down to the absolute minimum.

At times there may be some doubt about such redundancies. Are they real or merely the result of being too close to the material? In the presence of such doubt, the director must shoot his scene so that the final decision concerning possible deletions can be made in the cutting room. If several setups, including over-shoulder shots and close-ups, are available, deleting dialogue will present no problem for the editor. If, however, the scene is shot in one, a protection shot is necessary.

Protection shots are really a simple matter. A silent-reaction close-up of one of the scene's participants, ambiguous enough to be used over almost any speech, will usually furnish sufficient coverage.* If for some reason this kind of cut is not feasible, a

---

*From an audience point of view, no reaction shot is truly ambiguous. As

technique known in the cutting rooms as "cutting to the kitchen stove" can easily be applied. In plain words, a short cut of almost any object in the room or on the location can serve as a cutaway from the scene, during the course of which the desired deletion can be made. Such a cut may also earn the director a reputation as a profound symbolist, which brings up an interesting psychological point deserving of much more investigation than can be given it here.

As far back as 1920, Raymond Griffith, a leading comic of the silents, was working his way out of a desperate film situation.

"At this point in the fight," he said, "I reach under the bed, pull out this fire axe, and start chasing . . . "

"Whoa! Wait one minute!", cut in the director. "How does the audience know the axe is under the bed?"

"If they see me pull it out, they'll know it was there," was Griffith's answer. Of course, he did, and they did. An audience will accept as pertinent almost anything portrayed on the screen, even if it seems to make little sense. If it is there, the viewer assumes it must be there for a reason, and as often as not he will ascribe lack of clarity to his own lack of understanding. Used sparingly and with great care, this principle can be of considerable service to a troublesome scene or to a director who does not know what to do.

But back to the rehearsal. When dialogue, speech mannerisms, and length of scene have been put right and the actors are feeling at home with their roles and their lines, the pace of the scene must be carefully adjusted. Usually, this means speeding up the tempo, especially in relation to throwaways and overlapping lines of dialogue. It is an interesting aspect of film staging that the pace of an average scene must be measurably faster than that of an equivalent theatrical staging or, for that matter, real life. No one knows for sure why this is so, though some filmmakers have plausible theories, but so it is.

---

established in Kuleshov's well-known experiment, the viewer's reading of a neutral reaction depends to a very great extent on the shot to which the actor reacts. In other words, if they are truly involved, the viewers will supply their own interpretation. The wise director will use it.

Achieving an increased pace is a delicate operation. Overt pushing for greater speed leads only to scenes that appear rushed. The needed acceleration must be induced in so subtle a manner that the actors are not really aware that they have been coaxed into a faster pace.

An example can be taken from *The Young Lions.* In a "looping session," Monty Clift listened to a tape of himself speaking some lines. He looked puzzled and turned to me.

"That's not me," he said, ungrammatically and inaccurately.

"Of course it is," I assured him.

"It can't be," he protested. "I've never spoken that swiftly in my life."

I asked the projectionist to run the tape in sync with the matching picture. He did so and Clift was finally convinced, though he continued to shake his head in disbelief throughout the looping session.

It must be borne in mind that a scene that appears to be normally paced on the set may be dull as dishwater when seen at the rushes on the following day.

There are, of course, important exceptions to the general need for fast pacing, both in dialogue and in action. In a dialogue scene one looks for the moment of transition—that confrontation with an idea or bit of information that carries enough novelty, importance, or shock value to make the receiver of the information stop to think. It is the pause for thought that makes the scene come alive, both on the screen and in the mind of the viewer. Even as the character on the screen is forced to stop to regroup his thoughts or his attitudes under the impact of some unexpected or shocking statement, so the viewer is also marshalling his own reactions to the same information and forming new or stronger attitudes toward the film's characters. Thus it is often more important properly to gauge the length of time the viewer needs to digest the pertinent information than it is to be consistent within the scene itself. The exact timing for the actor's reactions can be achieved in the cutting room, but only if the director furnishes both himself and the editor the necessary material to play with.

Strange as it may seem, scenes of sharp or violent physical action frequently need to be slowed down. In a rather routine TV series made some years ago, starring Hugh O'Brien as Wyatt Earp, the final episodes dealt with the legendary gunfight at the O.K. Corral. The scenes of the battle, which actually lasted only a few seconds, were filmed in slow motion. Each combatant, whether firing a weapon, receiving a hit, or dodging one, was given full time on the screen. In other words, each of the many bits of action was separated from the whole, slowed down so it could be analyzed and understood, then rebuilt into the complete scene. The screen time involved was immeasurably greater than the real time of the original action, but for the first time the viewer could fully grasp the function and the fate of every gunman in the famous fight. Time stood still for the viewer, at least for long enough to engage his full attention.

The time differential in the cited example was exceptional and anticipated the effectiveness of the now commonplace instant replay used in sports broadcasting, but similar though less extreme techniques are often employed in filming action scenes. In shooting a prize fight, for instance, blows that are too quick for the eye to follow are slowed down to match the viewer's ability to grasp the action fully. The desired effect is not necessarily accomplished through the use of slow motion (now a rather trite technique); it is more often achieved by extending and overlapping the cuts used to show the fight. The same method can be used in shooting battle scenes, accidents, and other fast-paced events. In other words, film gives us the freedom to be in a number of places at the same time; "in the meantime" is an easily realized point of view. It is most important for the director to remember that one of the chief advantages of film as an art is this freedom to manipulate time as well as space, and it behooves him to learn how to use this special form of manipulation to maximum effect.

When the reading flows smoothly and the actors are at ease with their material and at one with their characters, movement rehearsals are in order. At this time it is customary for the director to outline roughly the players' starting positions and their preliminary moves. Although in this phase of the rehearsal the director may want to keep a somewhat tighter rein on the scene's development than he did at a similar stage in the reading, he may still find it fruitful to allow the actors a certain amount of creative freedom. As the rehearsals progress and the players settle into the scene, it becomes easier to modify, even restrict, their moves, since changes will present fewer threats and will be more easily accommodated.

Moves should always appear to be natural concomitants of the emotions and attitudes expressed in the scene. They should never be made simply to furnish action, nor should they be obviously choreographed. If a scene appears to be dull, the cause is almost certainly deeper than mere lack of action. The dynamics of a good scene, however, can be heightened by well conceived movement.

As previously mentioned, even the direction in which a movement takes place can contribute to a scene's vitality. Bringing an actor toward the camera, for instance, can affect the viewer's reception in two ways: first, by bringing him closer to the center of expression, the actor's face and eyes; and second, by gradually eliminating his awareness of the background as it goes out of focus and the actor's face takes over the greater part of the screen. A move away from the camera has the opposite effect, diminishing the presence of the actor while increasing that of the background and any action taking place in it. A move across camera does little beyond transporting the actor from one side of the screen to the other.

All this is extremely simplistic. It is mentioned only to give the student a starting point as his attention turns to setups. A number of these should have been visualized before the scene is rehearsed (a few as early as the first reading of the script) and some may still be valid. Except in the case of a highly stylized film, however, many camera positions may be modified because of the changes wrought during rehearsals.

Setups are a difficult area for the beginning director, and students often ask, "How do you determine where to put the camera?" That's easy. It is put where it will record what the director wants the viewer to see. *The director controls the viewer's attention.* It is largely a matter of instinct and experience. If a director's instinct is sound, his experience will be given the opportunity to grow; if not—well, there's always a place in his father's business.

At this point let us consider two basic problems that, despite their apparent simplicity, cause beginners and even a few old pros a disproportionate amount of agony. The first involves the question of size (as in long shot, medium shot, etc.), especially in a cutting context.

Quite obviously, cutting from one full-figure shot to another, similar full-figure shot will cause a "jump"—a distraction to the viewer—even though the setups are shot from different points of view. What is required, then, is a measurable difference in the figure sizes of the two contiguous cuts. In other words, one can cut from a full-figure to a close shot or from a close shot to a full-figure, but one should not cut from a full-figure to a calf-length shot—the size difference would not be marked enough to make the cut work smoothly. In this instance the cutting jump would not qualify as a desirable shock to the viewer; it would merely be undesirably disturbing. (The aforementioned stricture applies only to shots of the same person or persons. Shots of two different people not only can, but often should, be of the same size—for example, the separate, but similar, close shots of two people during a dialogue scene.)

There are exceptions, occasions when two similar-sized setups of one person, shot from decidedly different camera positions, can be smoothly juxtaposed, but they must be carefully composed with the cut in mind, and the cut itself must be made with the greatest finesse. The overwhelming majority of cuts involve two setups of distinctly different sizes—one more reason why the director should not only understand editing, but be able to keep the probable cutting sequence in mind as he shifts from setup to setup.

The second problem is one of direction, that is, the direction (screen right or screen left) in which an actor looks or moves. As an example, let us imagine a scene, a conversation between characters A and B. In the opening two shot (Figure 2) A is on the left of the screen looking at B, who is on the right side of the

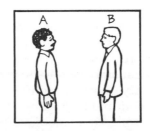

Figure 2

screen looking at A to the left. In their respective close shots, whether over-shoulder (Figures 3a and 3b) or individual (Figures 3c and 3d), their looks must remain consistent, that is, A should always look camera right and B should always look camera left, regardless of how sharply the camera diverges from its original two-shot position or how much the setup varies in relation to the set or any of the set pieces in it (see Chapter 7).

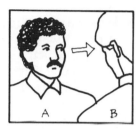

Figure 3a

Figure 3b

Figure 3c

Figure 3d

WRONG!
It appears that both are looking
off right – not at each other

Figure 3e

Figure 3f

If more than two people are included in the master setup, the direction problem becomes a great deal more complex. When filming a poker game, a board meeting, or a large family dinner, the question of consistent direction can tax the most mathematical mind.

Direction is also an important factor in exits, entrances, and any cross-screen movement that carries over from one cut to the next. If an actor exits a shot to the left side of the screen (camera left) (Figure 4a) and immediately walks into the next setup, he must enter the new shot from the right side of the screen (camera right) (Figure 4b). In other words, his movement must be consistently in one direction, in this case from right to left. A little thought will reveal why this requirement is of special importance in long, involved chases, rides to the rescue, and the like. It is needed to keep the action clean, consistent, and free of confusion. In effect, it shows our actor or actors going from here to there, or vice versa, and not from here (or there) to God knows where. It is sometimes permissible to mystify an audience or to surprise it, but to confuse it is completely unproductive and undesirable.

There are other, simpler effects that benefit from consistency in direction. For example, if the director wants a long shot of a plane flying from New York to London (Figure 5a), he will usually show it moving from left to right. The reason is quite simple; our maps show London to the right of New York, and the sight of a plane flying from right to left would be at least temporarily confusing. By the same reasoning, if we now cut to our actors inside the airplane (Figure 5b), their seats should face screen right, in the direction of the plane's movement. This rule is frequently

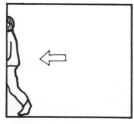

Figure 4a

Figure 4b

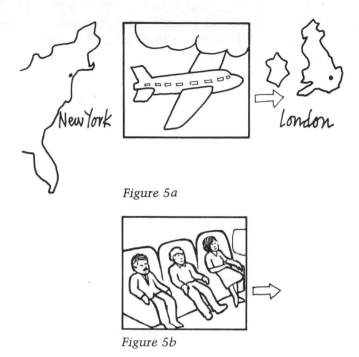

Figure 5a

Figure 5b

disregarded but, in general, unless there are pressing reasons for breaking it, it is wise to observe it faithfully.

Now a giant step backward. As the director watches the rehearsals in progress, he mentally reaffirms the scene's values, determines where he needs room or space, where concentration, where high emotional intensity, and where emotional relief. If the scene is one of action, he must decide whether to stage it in comprehensive full shots or in an integratable series of tight close shots.* Above all, he must keep in mind that the scene should not be looked at from a fixed position, as though seen on the stage. It is worth repeating that the camera can move in a 360-degree circle around the players, a fact too easily forgotten by those who have been conditioned by TV sitcoms.

---

*Note the shower murder scene in Hitchcock's *Psycho*, which consisted of nearly 100 close shots or inserts, none of which showed the knife entering the body.

By the time the scene is ready for filming, the director should know exactly what and how many setups are necessary to cover the scene thoroughly, and exactly how the final setup of the current shooting will lead into the first setup of the sequence to follow. Even as a chess master must be able to think a number of moves ahead, so the director must be able to visualize his setups to the end of each sequence and at least one setup beyond.

Most films contain at least one problem scene, a scene that fails to come alive, even though the dialogue, movement, and pacing appear to be dramatically correct. Such scenes can engender sleeplessness, gas pains, and prematurely gray hair. The causes of the problems vary and are difficult to discover—often, like Poe's "The Purloined Letter," because of their obviousness. I can only fall fack on an example, a scene whose problem, a contradiction in character, was easy to recognize but whose solution was not.

In *The Young Lions*, Dean Martin played an admitted coward, a man reluctant to lose his life in what he considered a useless war, who even deserted a friend to take a cushy noncombat job well behind the front. The plot made it necessary to get him back to his outfit, now fighting the enemy in France. In the script, he quarrels with his girlfriend in a London pub and, egged on by his own feelings of guilt, in a rash moment of pique he takes advantage of a general's presence to demand reassignment to his old unit.

The scene was well written, well rehearsed, and well played, but it didn't ring true. Martin's cowardly though likable character had been so well established that it was difficult to accept his sudden change of heart; it was completely illogical.

After repeated rehearsals, discussions, and coffee breaks, I was hit by a sudden inspiration, which like most inspirations, became instantly obvious. We were in a pub, so it was to be expected that Martin would have been drinking. The solution was something the script had not suggested, and I was slow in seeing— Martin was drunk! (If Martin had had his Las Vegas reputation in 1957 the solution might have been more easily arrived at.) Every viewer will accept the fact that a person under the influence of alcohol can do extremely illogical things. Not a line was changed, but the moment Martin's elbow slipped off the edge of the table in an uncoordinated tipsy move and his words came out slightly blurred, the scene became alive and believable.

"A director has to know when to leave his stars alone—to play, to relax, to get acquainted," Dmytryk says. Here Dean Martin and Montgomery Clift get relaxed for their party scene in **The Young Lions**.

It may relieve the reader to learn that when the director has succeeded in eliciting a fully satisfactory rehearsal, the worst is over. The next hour or two belongs to the cameraman and his crew as they light the set, and to the sound mixer as he fixes his optimum mike positions. When these craftsmen have completed their work, all that remains is to record the scene for posterity. This may take some time if actors falter or technical problems arise, but if the cast is truly professional, it will often be perfect the first time around. On the other hand. . . .

Some years ago, when low-budget films were a large part of every studio's output, many studios limited their B directors to a prescribed number of takes, usually four, in any one setup. This led to deception. After four unsatisfactory takes, the director would move his camera four or five inches, call it a new setup, and continue shooting the scene until it was played to his satisfaction or he ran out of time. In films made on a tight budget, takes and time are synonymous. Here again, the law of diminishing returns is brought into play.

The director may have a satisfactory take "in the can," yet feel that continued effort might result in something more nearly perfect. The actors, however, may be tired, dried up, or just not functioning perfectly at this particular time, and the shooting can go on and on. At some point, the director must decide if the cost in time and money is worth what little improvement might be gained, and if such improvement will really add measurable quality to the total worth of the film.

Another wasteful practice is the continued effort to get one perfect master shot when the director intends to cut the scene using several setups. If the director knows cutting and has visualized the cuts in the scene he is shooting, he need not, and should not, wait for the perfect and complete take. If the first half, let us say, of take 2 is well played, and the second half of take 6 is just right, and the director knows that somewhere in the middle of the scene he will use at least one cut from another setup, takes 2 and 6 of the original scene will serve to perfection, even though neither is completely perfect in itself. Further shooting is clearly a waste of time.

The same holds true for close-ups, two-shots, and so forth— any angles that will be intercut. The director need only remember which parts of which takes were usable. Then, referring to the script clerk's notes, he can pass the information on to his cutter.

Another consideration of importance is the relative return on the time spent in rehearsal and shooting versus the time spent in preparation and lighting. Too often the time required for the latter is so great that the actual shooting is rushed, to the detriment of the scene. This situation can only be improved by the understanding and cooperation of a competent cameraman.

Then there is a related problem: the preparation, lighting, and shooting of unnecessary setups, a sin more often committed than one would expect. Quite simply, if a director with a sixty-day schedule shoots twice the number of setups needed to cut the film properly, he is cheating himself of thirty days of his schedule, days that might have been productively used to improve those scenes eventually used in the film. I have known directors who actually overshot to this extent, but they were few. Most directors, however, are not as aware or as concerned as they should be, completely in their own interest. Quite obviously, all of a film's material and artistic resources should be spent on the scenes that will wind up in the film, not on the cutting room floor.

While set preparation and lighting are in progress, or even while the shooting is under way and the director is concentrating on the scene's quality or lack of it, part of his mind is concerned with the next setup—and the many others to follow. Even while he is dealing with the special problems of this necessarily fragmentary stage of filming, the director must bear in mind several requirements of the film as a whole.

One, already mentioned, is staggered flow of information. Another is tempo—not just the pace that contributes to a scene's vitality, but overall tempo of the film. This tempo may vary with the sequences even as it varies in the different movements of a symphony, but its general direction is up. Just as the range of an actor's physical movements should be modified as his image grows larger on the screen, to the point at which his body is motionless in a close-up, so the tempo of a film should increase as the viewer grows in awareness of story situations and in understanding of the film's inhabitants. When a viewer knows the film's characters well enough to be able to anticipate their reactions, those reactions should be curtly handled. It is only the unexpected action or reaction that needs to be dwelled on.

A third item of considerable consequence is the link. A film is a collection of a number of sequences made up of a greater number of scenes, which in turn, are created out of an even greater number of setups. Once recorded on film, these setups are called cuts. In most films it is imperative that one cut flows smoothly into another in a continuous array to form a scene; that each scene joins, apparently seamlessly, with those on either side of it to form a sequence; and that the sequences follow each other fluidly. The general idea is to keep the viewer's train of thought from jumping the track.

Necessary pacing and smooth linkage can be accomplished in the cutting room, but a better film will result if the director controls the pace and prepares the proper sequence springboards as he shoots. Naturally, this is difficult, since so much of the average film is shot out of sequence, but a cosmetic job done in the cutting room rarely approaches the perfection of proper timing achieved on the set. There just are not that many great creative editors around.

Dmytryk began his career as a film cutter, so he learned early what he wanted to see on film. He always told his cameraman exactly where to place the camera, and he never overshot. Here he is with one of his favorite cameramen, Harry Wild, in 1945.

10

Together at Last

Editing

Film editing or, as it is commonly called, "cutting," is unique. It is the one art or craft that is indigenous to motion pictures. All other film arts are borrowed or adapted. Stories and acting are as old as civilization, at least. So is music. Photography has its antecedents in pictorial art, and chemical means of recording images date back to the early ninteenth century. Film editing, which owes little except nomenclature to literary editing, was brought to life by motion pictures and it, in turn, brought motion pictures to life.

Film editing can be roughly divided into three categories: cutting, editing and montage. Of these, only montage is truly an art, although editing does at times reach that plateau. As it is understood today, montage is a limited technique in which a number of usually silent cuts are arranged, almost in collage form, to indicate the passage of time or occasionally, a manic or psychotic state of mind. In the last decade of the silent era, the Russians developed the technique into a high art that has not since been equaled.

While graciously giving credit to D. W. Griffith for initiating the technique, Russians like Eisenstein, Pudovkin, Kuleshov, and a few others developed montage into a special film form, although in this case necessity was certainly the mother of invention. The Germans, French, British, and Americans could tell their stories and make dramatic points with the help of printed titles; the inhabitants of the western world had a high degree of literacy. But 90 percent of the Russian people could not read, and thus titles were useless. Pictures had to say it all, and they did so most effectively; Eisenstein's *Potemkin* is still rated by many experts as the finest film ever made.

This distinctive technique was just beginning to blossom when it was nipped in the bud by the advent of sound. When films learned to talk, montage died and Russian films became as verbose and as dull as those of their political and artistic competitors—perhaps duller, since most of the mandated propaganda was difficult to dramatize.

Although the terms film cutter and film editor are commonly understood to be interchangeable, there is a definite, though informal, distinction. A cutter is a mechanic who learns a number of rather simple rules for cutting from one piece of film to another. He learns how to cut in movement, how to bring people into a scene or take them out of it, how to avoid making cuts that jump, that is, that are noticeable to the viewer. At best, he learns how to take the material given him and, following the director's scene selections and cutting instructions, how to build a smooth and properly paced film.

There was once a saying around the cutting rooms: A good cutter cuts his own throat. The implication was that in a well-cut film, cuts were unnoticed and so was the cutter's contribution. The ideal was to splice together thousands of pieces of film into a motion picture that the viewer would perceive as one continuous shot from beginning to end.

An unselfish ideal, surely, and one not too frequently realized or always respected. As a projectionist, I remember standing in the doorway of a cutting cubicle at Paramount Studios in which Josef von Sternberg was editing one of his films. At one point, Marlene Dietrich, looking over his shoulder into the moviola, tapped him for attention.

"That cut jumps," she said.

"I want it to jump," said Joe. "I want the audience to know there was a cutter on the picture—me."

Nevertheless, most cutters do their best to produce a fluid film, allowing cuts to jump only when some jolt to the viewer's sensibilities is called for, in which case, when properly executed, the jolt will register but the cut, or change of scene,* will still pass unnoticed.

To assure a properly finished film, one of two conditions must be met. The director must be a good cutter himself or he must employ a film editor who understands and shares the director's vision (gleaned largely from studying the script and watching the daily rushes with the director), and who is able to give the director what the man "wishes he had wanted," even though that director may have no technical knowledge of how cuts should go together.

The cutter's first duty is to deliver a version of the film, usually called the first cut, which the director expects to see. The assumption in that statement is that the director knows what he wants to see and, of course, good directors do, although only a few may have the necessary expertise to assemble such a version themselves. For this reason the relationship between the director and his cutter is a very special one. The latter is the former's right hand.

Ideally, the director should be an expert cutter or, better yet, a fine film editor. In spite of the time and effort spent in writing, preparing, and shooting the film, it has no shape or substance until the hundreds or thousands of bits and pieces that go to make it are assembled. Since there is an almost unlimited number of ways in which this can be done, the final result can be one of a large number of possible versions of varying quality. Only if the director knows how to put these bits and pieces together himself can his vision be completely realized. To put it simply, no director can claim to be an auteur unless he knows how to cut.

An in-depth discussion of cutting techniques and editing con-

---

*In film parlance, the word cut has several meanings, all easily understood in context. The verb to cut signifies the act of cutting together a number of scenes into a finished film or work print. Beyond that it serves as a noun in several contexts: first, meaning an unbroken strip of film recording part or all of a single setup; second, the splice or joint between two cuts of the first kind; third, to describe the total work print, especially when denoting the number of times the film has been reworked, as in rough cut, first cut, director's cut, final cut, etc.

cepts requires a book of its own. Here we can only consider a few of the problems the noncutting director may face. Perhaps the most difficult is one already mentioned in other contexts—objectivity.

At this stage of the filmmaking process the director may be too close to the picture. After months of living with it, it is difficult to know if the lines are real, if the characters are truly developed, or if the film as a whole has the hoped-for impact on a viewer who is not only seeing it for the first time, but who has no prior acquaintance with any of its aspects. Since the director "knows it all," too subjective a point of view may influence him to eliminate portions of the film he now finds stale, but that may be obligatory for audience understanding. The director must always place himself in the position of the viewer who is having his first look at the film. That is a difficult exercise. The process can be helped to a considerable degree if the director can manage to retain and recall the insights, understanding, and reactions he experienced on first being introduced to the story or the script.

More often, subjectivity brings a reverse effect. The story of Pygmalion is not an empty fable. Many creators fall in love with their creations, whether they be poems, pastries, or pictures. For very personal reasons they may become so enchanted with some facet of their work that they are oblivious to the audience's point of view, which may differ widely from theirs. Probably no good director, living or dead, has been completely free from this failing. A couple of examples may help to clarify the point.

Erich von Stroheim made a silent film for Paramount called *The Wedding March*. I was a young projectionist at the time, and had the privilege of showing him his first cut. It was 126 reels long without titles and took more than two working days to run. It was an exceptional exercise in montage and, from a technical point of view, an exceptional experience. But the average length of a film at that time was ninety minutes or less.

The Wedding March had to be chopped—and drastically—so von Stroheim and his cutter went to work. Some six months later the film was down to sixty reels, still five or six times the allowable length for release. Exercising its contractual option, Paramount took the film away from von Stroheim and assigned it to another cutter, who succeeded in reducing it to 24 reels. These were split into two films. The first, under the original title, was a complete flop. The second was never released in the United States.

Obviously, von Stroheim's delight in his creation was not shared by the general public. The original version might have thrilled a connoisseur, but such thrills must be communicable to a sizable audience or the whole purpose of commercial films is vitiated.

The preceding example is extreme; the next one is closer to us in time and experience. It involves Fred Zinneman's *High Noon*. Zinneman, too, found it impossible to get his film down to the length United Artists considered releasable, although in this instance the excess was nowhere near that of *The Wedding March*. He was reluctantly removed by Stanley Kramer, the producer, and the resulting shorter version of the film won a bagfull of Academy Awards, including one for Fred Zinneman.

In this case, Kramer's decision was debatable. If released today, when longer films are in vogue, Zinneman's version might have been an even better film—just maybe.

Few films are perfect. Almost all have troublesome spots, the number of these varying in inverse proportion to the film's quality. I have seen more films hurt by bad cutting than films saved by creative editing, but it is possible to create to advantage in the cutting room. This is where a good editor is of inestimable value. Once more I resort to examples by way of explanation.

George Nichols, Jr. was one of the very best film editors of his day. One of his assignments was a silent film version of the play *Heliotrope Harry*. In one segment of a suspenseful night sequence, a leading character makes his way down a dark alley in a shabby neighborhood and up a rickety flight of stairs to the door of a decrepit flat. Nichols decided he could add to the scene's suspense by appreciably increasing the length of the climb up the stairway, but the director had given him no extra setups to work with. Fortunately, there were several out-takes of the scene, all of which Nichols had printed. Seated at the moviola, he painstakingly checked each take, frame by frame, until he found one showing the actor on a lower step that matched a frame of the preceding cut, in which the actor was actually near the top of his ascent. Repeating the process with each of three or four consecutive cuts, he succeeded in contriving a "new" scene in which the actor seemed to be mounting a stairway several times the height of the original. The effort cost him eighteen hours of intense labor and the price of his first pair of eyeglasses, but the scene's suspense was considerably heightened, as was the director's gratitude.

Example number two: *Ruggles of Red Gap*, directed by Leo McCarey, starred Charles Laughton and Charlie Ruggles. Laughton had a rubber face and, though certainly a fine actor, was occasionally guilty of severe attacks of mugging, especially in moments of high emotional involvement. I was forced to cut around, or away from, much of his face making, but one sequence presented a nearly impossible problem. The scene was set in a western saloon. Laughton, playing Charlie Ruggles's very English butler (won in a poker game from a British lord), has accompanied his new boss to the bar. At one point, Ruggles wishes to quote from Lincoln's Gettysburg Address, but cannot remember the speech. Neither can any other member of his party or any of the saloon's habitues.

Suddenly, Ruggles's attention is arrested by Laughton, who is murmuring "Four score and seven years ago. . . . " Amazed to learn that the Englishman knows the words, Ruggles encourages him to continue.

Laughton was highly emotional and extremely nervous. Filming his shots alone, in medium close-up, occupied a day and a half. McCarey patiently shot the scene some forty or fifty times, rarely getting a complete take and never a perfect one. Finally Laughton, with tears streaming from his eyes, dropped to his knees and begged for mercy. McCarey decided to postpone further shooting.

At this point, I suggested that it might be possible to patch together a complete sound track by using the best parts of a number of takes. McCarey agreed. To begin with, I worked only with the sound track, checking out all of the fifteen or twenty printed takes, and an even greater number of out-takes. Using a line here, a phrase there, sometimes only a word or two, I pieced together a complete version of the speech. McCarey listened to it, liked what he heard, and asked me to complete it.

So far my efforts had been little more than routine. Now came the hard part. Fitting the picture to the track brought chaos, since each of the sound cuts needed a matching picture. Only one solution presented itself. The speech was started in a setup over Laughton's back, followed by cuts of the reactions of others in the saloon—first, Charlie Ruggles and his table companions, then other onlookers, as one by one they left their stools and walked over for a closer look and listen. Off screen, the butler's voice grew in strength as he gained confidence, and the speech ended triumphantly to the barkeeper's "Drinks on the house!"

Dramatic logic holds that at least a large part of the speech should have been played on the scene's central character, the butler. But every matching cut of Laughton showed his rather generous lips blubbering, his eyes turning upward in their sockets, and huge tears rolling down his cheeks. So, except for two short cuts, the entire speech was played over shots of the onlookers.

At the executive running, Ernst Lubitsch, then head of Paramount production, suggested that since the scene belonged to Laughton we should see more of him. McCarey agreed, and I was outvoted. I selected a pair of the most innocuous cuts and added them for the sneak preview.

Ruggles of Red Gap turned out to be one of that year's top films. At the preview it played beautifully—up to the Gettysburg Address. The scene started, players reacted, everything went well. Then came the first cut of Laughton, tears streaming down his cheeks as he spoke. Americans admire the Gettysburg Address, but they do not cry over it. The audience burst into laughter, which continued to build throughout the rest of the now inaudible speech. But laughter, at the expense of Lincoln's noble phrases, was not what we were looking for. One of the film's key scenes had been torpedoed.

As we left the theater after the preview, McCarey said, "Put it back the way you had it." I did, and the next preview confirmed our original judgment. This time there was no laughter. The audience listened attentively and applauded Laughton's performance. From that day until the end of Laughton's life, hardly a Lincoln's birthday passed without one of the major radio networks inviting him to once more deliver the Gettysburg Address.

Obviously, what an audience is not allowed to see can sometimes be as crucial as what it does see. This principle surfaces in a number of ways once the film reaches the cutting room. Further redundancies are now revealed that were not apparent on the set. A good deal of the cutter's polishing consists of eliminating them. At times, however, an opposite effort is required.

For instance, an actor's reaction to some line or action will prove inadequate as shot, and an addition to the start of the reaction is in order. If such a prelude to the actor's reaction is available in his close-up, there is no problem. Once in a great while, however, the footage available will be unsuitable, and a little ingenuity is called for. It may be possible, for instance, to find a close-up from another sequence that will do the trick. (If the shot is close enough the clothes and the background need not necessarily match.) In extreme cases, one can freeze a frame of film preceding the start of the actor's reaction for as much extra footage as is required. The actor's face will show no movement, of course, but immobility can also be a reaction, as in "He stood rooted to the ground in shock." If the movement immediately following the frozen footage is not too abrupt, the viewer will assume the scene was alive, even if unmoving.

Such extension or elongation of a reaction can result in a totally new or different meaning for the scene. For instance, if a man, speaking to a woman, says, "How about some soft music and some cool wine?", and her reaction is an immediate "All right," there is no apparent drama in the situation. But if her close-up shows her pausing an appreciable length of time as she studies his face and his invitation, the viewer can conceive of a number of possibilities and, more important, consequences that might be crossing her mind. Her eventual "All right," even though uttered with exactly the same intonation, shows a decision dramatically arrived at, and suggests a variety of future plot possibilities. As a rule, such acting decisions are made on the set, but once in a while alternatives are overlooked and can be inserted only during the editing process.

Many films are badly cut. Not all editing decisions are the result of constructive thinking. A common mistake is to assume that frequent cutting lends speed and vitality to a scene. That is by no means necessarily so. Such cutting more often results in a jerkiness of film line, which confuses the viewer and promotes the withdrawal of his attention rather than increased involvement. Action is no more a function of the multiplicity of cuts than it is the function of physical movement.

Dramatically speaking, movement takes place in the viewer's mind. A tight, exciting scene can be played in one setup by people in fixed positions and it can still move the audience as effectively as if it were played in a series of cuts—sometimes, in fact, it is more effective. The ideal is to give any scene exactly the amount of movement and the number of cuts that it needs and deserves or, as a mathematician might say, as are necessary and sufficient. But then, that is the basic requirement of any good dramatic scene.

Occasionally, the director may decide he wants an interchange of dialogue to proceed at a faster pace than it was originally played. Since the material for such manipulation is available if several setups have been shot, the speed-up can be easily achieved. Each speaker's lines are placed on a separate tape and timed to overlap, as if in interruption, the lines of the other speaker. The separate tapes are then recorded onto one master tape and the close-up images are matched to this recording. By using such a technique, the scene can be accelerated to breakneck speed if so desired or, on the other hand, slowed considerably if longer pauses for thought and reactions are required.

Another important editing consideration is the eventual addition of musical background. By intensifying dramatic involvement, music will often make a scene move faster. To take full advantage of this effect, the director should have a good idea of where such music is to be used. He can then afford to—indeed, he must—give the sequence a somewhat slower tempo, relying on the musical score to bring the scene up to the optimum pace. If such a sequence is cut to move at its ultimate tempo without music, the addition of the score may impart an unwelcome hurried appearance.

David Racksin, the composer, once said, "I have been told, 'We want to underscore this scene with a rendition of "The Marseillaise," ' but by the time the scene came out of the cutting room I could only play the anthem's first two bars—if I rushed them." Just one more thing for the director to consider while the cameraman lights the set.

All of these things and more can be achieved through the cutter's magic, but like all legerdemain it requires a lot of learning and much practice. No fledgling director can consider himself an editor on the basis of a semester or two of cutting exercises at some school of the cinema, and his demands for cutting rights are only asking for trouble and a botched-up picture. In recent years this has repeatedly been demonstrated by a string of costly mistakes that have spent a year or more in the studio intensive care unit, the cutting room.

Good cutting and skillful editing are most essential to good filmmaking. As noted, they can be achieved in one of only two ways: either the director finds and keeps an expert film editor as his alter ego, or he must determine to spend thousands of hours in the cutting room acquiring this vital craft.

In difficult locations, such as the windy heights of the Alps where much of The Mountain *was shot, sound recording of any quality is virtually impossible to achieve. Therefore, sound dubbing often has to be done once the film has been cut.*

11

Dressing it Up

Dubbing

Postediting is the time for mental convalescence. Major cutting is completed and the director can once more view the world through unguarded eyes. He can repair relationships that have become strained during production, reestablish friendships with members of the crew, and become reacquainted with his family. His job now consists of benign supervision, since the actual work is in the hands of experts whose contributions are largely dictated by the now-established form of the film. At this stage, many directors fade out of the scene, but the conscientious filmmaker will want to keep a measure of control to the bitter end.

It is at this stage that the producer comes back into the picture, and if the director slackens his hold on the reins, the producer is only to happy to pick them up. The knowledgeable executive may have some imput at the editing stage, though that usually occurs after the first preview. He may also want to join in the discussions concerning sound effects and music, which is the next phase of the production process.

The "sound running" comes first. As the term implies, the film is shown to the sound editor, the composer, and their assistants. To help in establishing an objective audience feel, the first run-through should always be continuous. This first viewing is immediately followed by a sequence-by-sequence review, with frequent stops to discuss the sound effects needed to flesh out or correct the working sound track. These effects can be as simple as door knocks, footsteps, sirens, or squealing tires, or as complex as the thousands of effects needed for a battle sequence, or as original as the new sounds required for modern science fantasies like *Star Wars*. Unless the director has some very special ideas in mind, most films are taken in stride by the sound editors.

Music is another matter, not nearly as cut and dried, and offering further opportunity for creativity. Even a director with a tin ear will usually insist on input into where and how much musical score is required. Normally, there is little disagreement concerning the amount or the placement of the music; nor, if the director (usually in collaboration with the producer) selects a composer with an established body of work, will there be differences of opinion concerning style.

A brief conference will quickly settle such matters, including the question of instrumentation. Do you want a full symphony orchestra, or would you rather opt for a single instrument? (Example of the latter: *The Third Man*, with a full score played on a zither.) Or do you settle for something between these two extremes? A great deal depends upon the content and style of the film, and some decisions may be crucial. Does a suspense sequence require dead silence, or eerie music? Will a battle scene play better against the background of a martial score, or will the stark, dramatic sounds of war supply a more effective mood? How about a theme song? Plenty of films have ridden to success on the popularity of their musical themes. In a few instances, these have been more financially successful than the films that gave them birth.

Such decisions require serious thought, but they rarely present serious problems, even if some of them are arrived at tentatively. When the composer has created (or borrowed) his themes for the film and its leading characters, he will play them for the approval of the director and the producer. Final decisions are made, and the composer continues with his work, leading up to the recording of the music.

In the meantime, the cutter or the sound editor has been preparing tapes (and picture, where used) for looping. Looping is the process of recording new dialogue to replace that which is indistinct or inaudible, usually because of the presence of excessive background noise. Almost every film will require some looping; a few that have been shot on noisy locations, such as busy streets, may have most of their dialogue replaced. Even night shooting in a desert countryside may surprise the sound engineer with a deafening cricket chorus that will drown out the players' voices.

Some directors charge their cutters with the responsibility of looping, but this practice is indefensible on any production of quality. The dialogue recorded in a looping session should be as good dramatically as the original, and if that needed the director's guidance at the shooting stage, so it does when looping. Only the director can know if he is getting the quality that the film demands.

The most common looping technique employs both sound and picture. Duplicate prints of the scenes to be looped are cut into short segments, usually consisting of no more than a line or two of dialogue. The tape is cued with a rhythmically timed series of beeps before the start of the dialogue; the picture usually carries a scribed line, or scratch, also zeroing in on the instant the player starts to speak. Each segment is reviewed in its turn for pace and intonation until the actor feels ready to perform, at which time his words are recorded on clean tape. The selected takes of each line of dialogue are then used to replace the original "dirty" versions.

My preferred technique uses only the sound tape. It is much faster, easier on the actors, and a good deal more accurate and acceptable. For this method, the dialogue is cut into the shortest possible phrases—the shorter, the better—and separate loops are made of each phrase. When recording, the actor listens to the loop as often as necessary, depending on the complexity of the phrase. When he is ready to record, the recorder is turned on, the actor hears the original words, and then, in the few seconds of silence that follow on each loop, he repeats them—mimics them, really. He must capture the original rhythm, intonation, and emotion, which is not difficult if the phrase is short enough. The loop repeats the original dialogue as often as necessary for the actor to give the most satisfactory reading.

This technique achieves the best reproduction of the original dialogue, as well as the most accurate synchronization. The director must take care, however, to shoot the original scene properly, regardless of background noise, in order to obtain a "cue track" that carries the proper intonations and emotions. Only then can the looping supply comparable quality to the dubbed scene.

More sophisticated electronic techniques for looping do exist but, due either to higher costs or greater studio inflexibility, these systems are rarely if ever used.

Film colonies in all countries include actors known as looping specialists. These artists are especially useful when a film is dubbed into a foreign language or when, as frequently happens in international productions, some of the local actors cannot manage English satisfactorily. These specialists usually command a number of accents or dialects, often enabling them to dub a number of different roles in the same film, and they are very skillful at lip synching.* It pays to be aware of their existence and their talents.

During the preparation for the final "mix," occasional checks of sound effects and music will be called for, but they will not be a major concern to the director until the music is to be recorded. Usually, recording sessions flow smoothly, but problems can arise, and settling differences at this time is more useful, and certainly more economical, than calling additional recording sessions after the sneak preview.

The postediting activity, which may take from six weeks to several months, culminates in the dubbing, or rerecording, session. Depending on the quality and difficulty of the sound effects, and the speed and skill of the sound engineers (or mixers) the session will last for a week or two on the average. This is concentrated, eight-hours-a-day work—sometimes longer—and the director should devote his full energy and attention to this phase of filmmaking.

Most artists harbor some bias in favor of their own fields and with the best of intentions, self-interest can creep into the film at this point. Perhaps the composer would like to hear just a touch more of his music, which may just possibly cover or dirty up an important bit of dialogue. Or, in a scene demanding heavy and complex sound effects, the urge that motivates the composer

---

*Lip synching is timing the recorded dialogue with the lip movements of the actor as the latter appear on the screen.

may also affect the sound editor. These tendencies are normal, often desirable, and certainly not to be criticized, but they do have to be carefully controlled. For instance, in a dramatic scene shot against a noisy background, the director may want to diminish or even eliminate the sound effects once the scene has captured the attention of the audience, and its awareness of the noise disappears as its emotional involvement in the scene increases.

As a rule, only the director can objectively maintain a sense of the proper balance of the values involved in the mix.* If he ignores this important aspect of filmmaking, he risks having a final result not exactly to his taste.

Of course, corrections are usually in order after the sneak preview, but if improvements are to be made, it is always better to move from excellent to perfect than from fair to good.

---

*In my entire film experience I have known one mixer whose creative vision was such that I would have trusted his judgment on the proper mix for any of my films. His feeling for dramatic balance bordered on genius. But, like many another genius, John Cope died at an early age.

Sneak previews can be valuable indicators of how a film can be improved before commercial release—but beware. A blue collar town that loves Westerns and war movies might not provide the most objective reaction to such films as **Anzio**.

12

Let's Get it Out!

The Preview

Objectivity! the sneak preview demands it in its purest form. Even the term implies it. Why "sneak?" To minimize the possibility of an "in" audience—a studio claque. At its best the sneak can provide valuable insights into the film's relative values; at its worst, it can be a trap of self-centered deceit. The trap is set at the very beginning, with the selection of a theater and its audience.

It is quite likely that every theater within a 500-mile radius of Hollywood has been pegged, that is, the smart producer or director knows what kind of an audience patronizes each house. Each will be considered friendly, neutral, or tough, classified by the average age of its patrons, the presence or lack of audible reaction to humor (and what kind of humor), its drama absorption rate, its philosophic or religious outlook, and by its level of sophistication.

Darryl Zanuck refused to preview dramatic films on the ground that, "If I don't know more about drama than the average preview audience, I shouldn't be running a film studio." A classic example of asking for it, but Zanuck was probably right.

Musicals and comedy in most of its forms are different kettles of fish. A gag that brings gales of laughter in a studio projection room may leave an audience cold. Since in their early stages most musicals contain numbers in excess (because of creative uncertainty), an audience will quickly register its order of preference and indicate where obvious deletions should come.

What is the director's purpose in choosing a particular preview audience? Does he want his film to play well to impress the producers and the executives? If so, he will choose a friendly theater, whose audience will spark at the mere sight of the title announcing "A major studio preview," will laugh easily and long, and will view the film without cynicism or hostility. This type of audience will turn in a large majority of favorable preview cards even if the film is an unpretentious B movie.

If the film's action or comedy is based on car crashes, unbridled destruction of property, and violence, the director will opt for an audience of high school and college students. If it carries a religious slant, he will sneak it in the nearest farm community; if it promotes a liberal message, it will be shown in a university setting or a minority community. If it is heavy drama, a theater catering to an older audience will be selected.

If, on the other hand, the director seeks an honest, even a hard evaluation, he will choose a theater known for its tough or cold audience. After all, a truly humorous sequence will play well with any audience, young or old, though too much sophistication may misfire in the Bible belt. A solid dramatic scene, containing no "corn" or "soap" will get across to viewers of almost any age or background.

Preview cards are distributed to audiences at all sneaks. These cards ask the viewer to evaluate the film from poor to excellent. As in all straw polls, there are pitfalls. At a well-attended showing in a moderate-sized neighborhood house, the studio can expect a harvest of from three hundred to four hundred cards. Of these, a few from ultragenerous viewers will rate it, "The best I've ever seen!" At the opposite pole on the generosity scale, another five or ten will say, "It stinks!" Obviously, both extremes should be discarded. The rest can be considered more or less objective and should be so analyzed. But are they? Not as a rule.

One of the more curious but perfectly natural postpreview phenomena is each craftsman's interpretation of the audience reaction. A good comedian could probably do a ten-minute routine on each person's remarks as the studio contingent seeps out into the theater lobby after the screening. The sound mixer will say, "It *sounded* great!" The cameraman will comment on the quality of the print. The composer will like his music, but wish for "a little more 'presence' during the love scene." The cutter will be pleased that the cuts did not jump and will want to make a few more snips. An actor, if present, will usually be somewhat self-critical. The executives, as always, though exuding optimism, will suggest that the film could "lose fifteen minutes without hurting anything."* If the film has played well, the director will be euphoric—a great load has been lifted. If the film has not played well, he will call his agent and urge him, "Get me one to recoup on before this one is released."

Another curious phenomenon is that twenty "fair" cards will outweigh a hundred "very good" ones. Studio executives especially, are always more reactive to one adverse opinion than to ten that are favorable. The very old-fashioned and palpably unrealistic attitude that a good film should be unanimously loved still exists in the minds of many distributors and exhibitors. That is not only improbable, it is impossible. I first learned the bitter lesson as a B director.

The film, a Karloff stapel called *The Devil Commands*, was previewed at an exceptionally friendly theater in Inglewood. The house was packed. The introductory title, "This is a major studio preview," elicited the usual anticipatory applause. Then came the first main title card—Boris Karloff in *The Devil Commands*. There was a chorus of descending "Ahs." Half the audience got up and walked out. I was devastated. For a few moments I blacked out mentally. When I could think rationally again, I realized that if I had been only a viewer I, too, whould have left the theater, since I never went to see Karloff movies. It had nothing to do with the ability of the actor or the quality of the film—not one of those leaving the theater had seen a foot of it. It simply meant that those people did not spark to Karloff as a primary star or to that type of horror film. It they had walked out in the middle of

---

*It took me years to discover they were not concerned so much with the film's pace as with the shorter running time, which would allow them to coax one more audience per day into the theater. Some fine films have been weakened by this policy.

the movie we would have been in trouble. But such a film appealed only to Karloff fans, of whom there were enough in the world at large to make Columbia a neat profit if it were produced at a controlled cost. It was and it did.

Another example: Some years ago, M-G-M produced one of Hollywood's greatest films, *Doctor Zhivago*. The nation's leading news weeklies, *Time* and *Newsweek*, reviewed it. One considered it a truly great film, the other saw it as the decade's disaster. If these intelligent, sophisticated, knowledgeable critics could have such an extreme divergence of opinion, what can one expect from a preview audience composed of average citizens?

In truth, preview reactions are most useful when analyzed piecemeal, and not as a whole. It is quite possible the audience will pinpoint faults that those close to the film have overlooked (sometimes due to wishful thinking). For instance, if it is a drama, does the viewer feel it is too long? Is he bored? And is it too long, or does it simply lose its audience, making it seem so? This could be the result of one or more of a number of factors other than running time.

Is it completely and continually understandable? If not, the shortcoming might be due to obscure writing, inept staging, or surprisingly often, lack of clarity in the dialogue spoken by a foreign star whose command of English is not too secure or by an English-speaking actor who equates slovenliness of speech with realism.

Is the pace too slow, allowing the viewer's attention to wander? That fault can probably be corrected in the cutting room.

Are the characters properly developed? There have been instances where, for the sake of an upbeat tempo, character development has been sacrificed in favor of action, resulting in the loss of audience interest. If the characters are not sufficiently developed, neither is the viewer's empathy.

Are some of the lines overly dramatic? Melodramatic dialogue is corny, and corn will usually elicit horse laughs rather than emotional reaction.

The question of laughter applies to drama and melodrama as well as comedy. There should be some relief or release in the starkest of films. But laughs should be studied and understood. There is more than one kind of laughter, especially from film audiences. There is the chuckle, the snicker, the warm laugh, the hearty laugh, the "belly" laugh, the "horse" laugh, and an assortment of others less common. These are sometimes hard to distinguish or interpret. It is even harder, in the case of bad laughs, to analyze the cause and remove it. But it can be done (see Chapter 10).

Comedy laughter is not too difficult to analyze. There is good and frequent laughter, there is good but infrequent laughter (some trouble brewing), there is no laughter (deep trouble), or there are horse laughs (put it on the shelf). The director should be aware, however, that laugh scenes in a film must be handled differently from such scenes in the theater. On the stage an actor can wait for the laugh, or continue quickly if none is forthcoming. In a film, the actor and the director are in the dark, even after a preview, since not every subsequent audience will react in the same way—a fact of life every comedian has learned. In films, the technique of choice was pioneered by the Marx Brothers, who piled laugh upon laugh in rapid-fire order. A viewer might miss a number of gags because they were covered by laughter carrying over from the previous lines, but he could come back for another showing, sit close to the screen, and catch the missed dialogue, which is exactly what a gratifyingly large number of viewers did.

Not to be overlooked is the mechanical preview, in which the audience reaction is recorded on a graph and coordinated with the picture. If the audiences are well chosen as to cross section of the movie population, the graph will be remarkably similar for every running of the film, even though the make-up of the audience changes with each viewing. An obvious advantage of this technique is that low points of interest are objectively recorded, leaving little room for argument based on personal reaction or wishful thinking. Filmmakers who truly seek to eliminate subjective judgment, either by themselves or by others, will usually opt for the mechanical preview.

Some films, either because they are very good or hopelessly bad, require only one preview; others may need several, with changes being made between showings to correct revealed faults. At last, even these come to an end, and the director can let go— except for one final moment of agony, the press preview. The ultimate judge, of course, is the audience for whom the film is made, but the critics find that hard to accept. Based on their own individual reactions, they will rip a work to pieces or praise it to the skies. Either way, the director's ego is in great danger.

Eddie Dmytryk rests a moment between takes while shooting Anzio.

Postscript

Beyond the immediate area of techniques necessary for intelligent filmmaking in general, there is much special, even unique, information that must be researched and acquired for each separate film. Perhaps one of the most attractive aspects of filmmaking is the opportunity it affords—no, demands—for seeking and gathering special knowledge in discrete fields.

Unless the director chooses to limit himself to a single genre, he will, in the course of a normal career, make films depicting characters living and working in a variety of historical periods and physical and social environments. If he is to do justice to these films, he must spend considerable time in researching and studying the place, period, environment, and population involved in each one.

For instance, if the director is to make a serious, adult Western, he must study the area of the country and its inhabitants as they really were, not as presented in myth (although the myth will also reward serious consideration). A Civil War film will require a careful study of the period, of northern and southern economic and social structures, armaments of the time, and so on. A modern war film will, if it involves land fighting, necessitate learning a good deal about Army organization, personnel, and tactics, as well as the history of the particular war. The knowledge and information so gained will be of little use, however, if the director then makes a Navy film. The history, education, attitudes and philosophies, and personalities of the men in the two services vary to such a great extent that a completely new study would be required. (Incidentally, the director of such a film will benefit immensely if he takes the time to view the hundreds of thousands of feet of stock material available at the respective service archives.)

Filming in foreign countries means acquiring at least a working knowledge of the native tongue, as well as an awareness of the history, culture, and social customs of the country in question.

During the actual filming, the director will always have the assistance of one or more technical experts, which is not necessarily an unmixed blessing. It has been my experience that one technical expert is not always right, as a second technical expert will be only too happy to testify. Since the director is the arbiter in any dispute, technical or otherwise, a certain amount of discreet double-checking may be needed. In any event, it behooves the director to acquire as much knowledge as he can in all the areas his film covers.

For ten years I was a film editor at Paramount, the only Hollywood studio that assigned its cutters to the set, there to help with editorial and setup decisions—if the director invited such assistance. Throughout the thirties I worked with some of that decade's best filmmakers. Actually, since many of them were extremely protective of their images, I spent most of my time on the set watching, listening, and occasionally wrestling (in my mind, of course) with some problem confronting the director. Eventually, I found myself winning the fall more often than losing it and, with the cockiness of youth, I grew to feel I knew most of what there was to know about filmmaking.

What a shock to discover that although I had learned a good deal about the technical and mechanical aspects of directing, I had been aware of only a very small part of what went on in the directors' minds. Processes involved in the making of their creative decisions had never been openly discussed. I now know that no such discussion was possible, except in the most general terms. If any person could pass on the ability to recognize and take advantage of creative opportunities by any means other than possibly genetic, the world would be crowded with creators, which would mean we would have no creators at all.

Although it is true that talent cannot be taught, it can be made more aware, and it is only in the area of awareness that this book is meant to wander. To increase that awareness, a truly dedicated film student will do a great deal of outside reading. Herewith, some suggestions addressed to the aspiring director (no specific authors, since there is a mountain of material in all the recommended categories, only subject matter):

To understand the architecture of the screenplay, you must study not only the best films, past and present, but the structures of the novel, the short story (especially apropos because of its ability to develop character and situation in a limited amount of space and time), and musical composition, since its techniques of pacing, emphasis, prestatement, and development of theme parallel good film structure to a surprising degree.

To understand the character of man, the subject matter should be anthropology, animal behavior, and sociobiology. To understand what shapes the minds of characters and establishes their standards, study philosophy and religion—all religions. To understand what minds, so conditioned, have done with their world, look into history.

On a more practical level, to obtain hints on audience manipulation and to learn how to draw the most and the best out of both crew and cast, study psychology, of course.

Above all, study the world around you, and the people in it—all people, the short and the tall, the thin and the fat, the beautiful and the ugly, the biased and the generous of mind—but especially, the "average." Most craftsmen can make some kind of dramatic fare out of the extremes, but if you can uncover those elements that touch the heart, and make high drama out of the "ordinary," you will be an artist indeed.

Filmography
of
Edward Dmytryk

THE HAWK   (Ind)   (1935)
TELEVISION SPY   (Para)   (1939)
EMERGENCY SQUAD   (Para)   (1939)
GOLDEN GLOVES   (Para)   (1939)
MYSTERY SEA RAIDER   (Para)   (1940)
HER FIRST ROMANCE   (I.E. Chadwick)   (1940)
THE DEVIL COMMANDS   (Col)   (1940)
UNDER AGE   (Col)   (1940)
SWEETHEART OF THE CAMPUS   (Col)   (1941)
THE BLONDE FROM SINGAPORE   (Col)   (1941)
SECRETS OF THE LONE WOLF   (Col)   (1941)
CONFESSIONS OF BOSTON BLACKIE   (Col)   (1941)
COUNTER-ESPIONAGE   (Col)   (1942)
SEVEN MILES FROM ALCATRAZ   (RKO)   (1942)
HITLER'S CHILDREN   (RKO)   (1943)
THE FALCON STRIKES BACK   (RKO)   (1943)
CAPTIVE WILD WOMAN   (Univ)   (1943)
BEHIND THE RISING SUN   (RKO)   (1943)
TENDER COMRADE   (RKO)   (1943)
MURDER, MY SWEET   (RKO)   (1944)

BACK TO BATAAN   (RKO)   (1945)
CORNERED   (RKO)   (1945)
TILL THE END OF TIME   (RKO)   (1945)
SO WELL REMEMBERED   (RKO–RANK)   (1946)
CROSSFIRE   (RKO)   (1947)
THE HIDDEN ROOM   (English Ind.)   (1948)
GIVE US THIS DAY   (Eagle-Lion)   (1949)
MUTINY   (King Bros.–U.A.)   (1951)
THE SNIPER   (Kramer–Col)   (1951)
EIGHT IRON MEN   (Kramer–Col)   (1952)
THE JUGGLER   (Kramer–Col)   (1952)
THE CAINE MUTINY   (Kramer–Col)   (1953)
BROKEN LANCE   (20th-Fox)   (1954)
THE END OF THE AFFAIR   (Col)   (1954)
SOLDIER OF FORTUNE   (20th-Fox)   (1955)
THE LEFT HAND OF GOD   (20th-Fox)   (1955)
THE MOUNTAIN   (Para)   (1956)
RAINTREE COUNTY   (MGM)   (1956)
THE YOUNG LIONS   (20th-Fox)   (1957)
WARLOCK   (20th-Fox)   (1958)
THE BLUE ANGEL   (20th-Fox)   (1959)
WALK ON THE WILD SIDE   (Col)   (1961)
THE RELUCTANT SAINT   (Col)   (1961)
THE CARPETBAGGERS   (Para)   (1963)
WHERE LOVE HAS GONE   (Para)   (1964)
MIRAGE   (Univ)   (1965)
ALVAREZ KELLY   (Col)   (1966)
ANZIO   (Col)   (1967)
SHALAKO   (Cinerama)   (1968)
BLUEBEARD   (Cinerama)   (1972)
THE HUMAN FACTOR   (Bryanston)   (1975)